THE
THREE-MINUTE
PHILOSOPHER

Also by Fabrice Midal

C'est La Vie: The French Art of Letting Go

THE
THREE-MINUTE
PHILOSOPHER

Inspiration for Modern Life

FABRICE MIDAL

ORION
SPRING

First published in Great Britain in 2021 by Orion Spring
an imprint of The Orion Publishing Group Ltd
Carmelite House, 50 Victoria Embankment
London EC4Y 0DZ

An Hachette UK Company

1 3 5 7 9 10 8 6 4 2

Translated by: Austin Dean and Team SLA
Special thanks for the translation go to: Austin Dean, Helena Sandlyng-
Jacobsen, Noa Rosen, Mark Kessler, Kerry Glencorse and Susanna Lea

Originally published as 3 Minutes de Philosophie pour Redevenir
Humain by Editions Flammarion/Versilio in France in 2020.

A CIP catalogue record for this book is
available from the British Library.

ISBN (Hardback) 978 1 3987 0178 6
ISBN (eBook) 978 1 3987 0180 9

Typeset by Born Group
Printed and bound in Great Britain by Clays Ltd, Elcograf S.p.A.

www.orionbooks.co.uk

Contents

INTRODUCTION

Philosophy takes us by surprise. It challenges us; awakens us and opens our minds. That's why we need it so badly.

Nowadays, philosophy is more important than ever because it's the antithesis of the rampant dogmatism that dominates so much public discussion, of the vehemently expressed opinions of those who think they know everything and want you to agree with them.

Socrates, the father of Western philosophy, insisted that he was an expert in . . . nothing. He would stand in public and ask everyone questions, about their life, their profession, their tastes. He didn't try to sermonise. He explained that he himself knew nothing, that he wasn't even a 'sage', a term that only applied to the gods, if they existed. He explained that it is pointless to aspire to being wise. Instead, we should focus on what it is that makes us human. For, in so doing, we have everything to gain.

Philosophy does not tell us to be 'wise', to be perfect or godlike, but instead to nurture our own humanity.

And this is why Socrates asked questions, why he dared challenge the seemingly obvious and indisputable. He wanted to open our eyes. To give us confidence in our capacity to feel, to think and to love. As this is what philosophy teaches us: the value of exploring our own experiences in depth.

Self-proclaimed 'experts' tell us to listen to and obey their injunctions, while philosophers encourage us to think for ourselves.

For several years, I have been trying to understand the new forms of daily aggression that weigh on us and distance us from our humanity, our convictions and aspirations. Whether you're a nurse, a doctor, a baker, a lawyer or a social worker, you might feel the same way as I do: that we are often asked to do something that doesn't make sense, for social, political or economic reasons. We convince ourselves that we're not doing enough and we push ourselves to the point of burnout.

Philosophy can help us precisely because it does not tell us to be calmer or to be perfect, to be like a robot or an algorithm. It encourages us to be human.

The following chapters each take only three minutes to read. Three minutes to reconnect with your humanity and free yourself from the brutal diktats of the constant need to perform. Philosophy addresses what makes us human and it helps us to navigate everyday life: from dealing with an annoying colleague at work, to the panic on realising that your fridge is empty when guests arrive out of the blue. When our lives feel increasingly abstract, philosophy is a very concrete tool.

I have chosen quotes that do justice to Socrates' genius in that they do not necessarily come from the traditional canon of philosophy but from a range of artists, thinkers and writers. We do not always find philosophy where we expect to and that is why it is both beneficial and necessary.

'THE ESSENCE OF BEING
HUMAN IS THAT ONE DOES
NOT SEEK PERFECTION'
GEORGE ORWELL

Simply being human

Orwell not only asks us to realise that there's no such thing as perfect, but that to seek perfection is to turn our backs on what it means to be human.

This is an unsettling statement. For centuries, all schools of thought had us seeking out perfection, a sort of detached state, or the victory of reason over everything else. And so, it's true, we'd all like to be a little more perfect! We think that we would be happier if we were. We are wrong.

You were a little too aggressive with your brother-in-law

You realise that you've said inappropriate, even hostile, remarks to someone you care about. For example, during a family dinner, you laid into your amiable brother-in-law just because you were annoyed that he didn't agree with your politics. And now you regret it. This is a good sign! You are tapping into a deeper side of your existence.

Instead of blaming yourself again and again for not living up to your own idea of perfection – someone who is always fair and in control – you're facing the abyss of your own heart. This allows you to stop being hard on yourself and to show yourself some compassion. Yes, sometimes you're clumsy, inept and you can be a bit of an idiot.

Do you know what makes a great writer? It's the ability to reveal the part of us that is petty and mediocre. This is the genius of Dostoyevsky or Proust. They reveal all of the twists and turns of our lies, our cowardice and jealousy . . . They don't do this out of cruelty or desperation but rather so that we may grasp what makes up the profound reality of our existence. And it is calming to finally be able to recognise the complexity but also the beauty of our lives. Bad writers only scratch at the surface of our feelings – their false promises of happiness are insufferable.

Good writers are moved by an infinite sense of tenderness that allows them to view human beings in all of their dimensions. Bad writers don't do this because they are afraid. They are afraid of real life. They are afraid of their own hearts.

A meditation on a slightly cracked Japanese pot
How do we make peace with our imperfections? Think about someone you love. Think about their faults, their

wounds. Consider these faults not as something that holds them back but rather as what makes them beautiful.

Think about the works of the great Japanese master potters. Once they had finished making a bowl, they would add a flaw, not to defile or damage it, but as an expression of both the fragility and humility of creation. To know that we ourselves are imperfect makes us more tolerant and caring towards others.

'IN THE MIDST OF WINTER,
I DISCOVERED THAT THERE
WAS WITHIN ME AN
INVINCIBLE SUMMER'
ALBERT CAMUS

Stop putting everything in perspective

We're used to thinking that summer follows winter, that joy follows pain, that sunshine follows rain. If you're feeling bad, don't worry because someday it'll be better. This is what conventional wisdom teaches us. Essentially, this forces us to put everything into perspective. However, I've found that this isn't enough.

Camus invites us to explore a whole new perspective: we should learn to realise that even in the middle of winter, in the middle of a time that is icy and devoid of life, the teeming presence of summertime is there. Think about the following possibility: there are no happy or sad events per se but with each event, in every moment of our lives, there's a deeper dimension.

You've just lost a loved one

I experienced this when my grandmother, whom I loved dearly, passed away. She was very old and we had known for a while that the end was coming. One morning, my aunt called to warn me that Mamie was in her final hours. When I reached the hospital, my whole family was there, speaking with hushed voices in the hallway. It was an incredibly fraught moment. One by one, family members solemnly entered Mamie's room and left overwhelmed with emotion.

When it was my turn to go in, I was nervous. I took the time to sit down and be present with my grandmother. To my surprise, I could feel her kindness, the same kindness that enveloped me throughout my childhood. I stayed all day long in that room and could feel a poignant and profound sense of peace. I knew that, somehow, I was helping her through her final moments of suffering.

Of course, I was terribly sad that she was dying – but I could feel intensely, in the middle of this winter, the beauty of the love that she had never stopped giving me. It remains one of the most important moments of my life. It gave me a strength and confidence that I still carry with me today.

A meditation on finding your secret friend within

But how can we have this revelation every day? It's not enough just to find a ray of sunshine in the middle of winter, we must find an invincible summer that can never be vanquished. A summer that always lives within us, without having to replace or blot out winter.

It's there, like a dear friend, a friend we've forgotten, who we lost touch with a long time ago. This forgotten friend lives within your soul, inside your heart, in your chest, in your body's every cell. It's made up of your memories and of everything you've learned in life. It's the love that your grandmother, or someone else, gave you. You can offer this forgotten friend your hand and tell them: 'My neglected friend, I turn to you as my first ally, to form a bond of friendship, peace and trust. I confide in you and rely on you, for you are a part of me that is bigger than me.'

'IT IS TIME THAT THE
STONE MADE AN EFFORT
TO FLOWER'
PAUL CELAN

Learning to open up

How can something that is closed open up? How can something that seems dead become alive? This is what Paul Celan, one of the most dazzling poets of the 20th century, invites us to discover.

This promise seems extraordinary but also improbable. Think of a stone. It's solid, unmoving. Of course, it is unable to flower. Isn't this line a perfect example of poetry capturing sentiments that are certainly beautiful but totally unrealistic?

But let's not be too hasty. Paul Celan is offering us an experience so profound that it deserves some attention.

You can't fall asleep

To understand Celan's message, let's think about sleep.

Have you ever had a hard time falling asleep or struggled with insomnia? If you have, you know that wanting to fall asleep is not enough. On the contrary, the more you want to sleep, the less likely it is to come. You feel like a stone that nothing could bring to flower. For sleep to carry you away, you need to trust your body. Your body wants nothing more than to sleep, but your will is holding you back.

That's the key!

We mistakenly think that we need to try harder: if we're anxious, we should do something about it; if we suffer from addiction, we need more willpower to overcome it; if we procrastinate, it's because we lack self-discipline.

But this is all wrong. And because he knows that, Paul Celan invites us to surrender to the life that is there, hidden in the stone of our sorrows, which lies latent and imperceptible.

This lesson applies to many other areas.

For a long time, Cézanne painted very heavy, clumsy works. He would later refer to it as his *période couillarde*, his crude or 'ballsy' period. And then, one day, the stone flowered.

No one can know exactly why. Cézanne simply trusted completely in his painting.

It's time for the stone to give in to the impossible, for life to return to where it had been shut out. It's time to free that which is blocked. This process demands patience and trust.

A meditation on trust

Would you like to have a go? It's very simple. Let yourself for a moment know nothing, decide nothing. Allow yourself to stay just where you are.

Letting go is something that's long been overlooked – it means letting life take its course and come to you, like when you have a cut and all you can do is wait for it to form a scab and heal over. This is trust.

At first, this can seem a bit ridiculous. But you must start here in order to appreciate the great blessing of trusting something about which you cannot be absolutely certain. If I trust in what you tell me, it's precisely because I can't be absolutely certain of it. And that's the whole beauty of life.

'ONE MUST LEARN NOT BY
THE EXAMPLE OF WISE MEN,
BUT BY THAT OF CHILDREN'
EMIL CIORAN

Abandon the idea of being wise

Being wise, we believe, means always being in control, never allowing ourselves to get carried away. This notion comes largely from the Stoics and in particular from Epictetus, who has come to embody the ideal of self-control and reserved wisdom.

A famous anecdote has come to epitomise Epictetus's disposition: once, when Epictetus was a slave, his master started twisting and bending the philosopher's injured leg. Epictetus said to him, 'If you keep doing that, my leg is going to break.' His master continued contorting his leg until the bone snapped. Instead of howling in pain, Epictetus simply said, 'I warned you.' He stayed serene and stoic, completely unfazed.

Well, I don't believe in such damaging wisdom. It's time we got rid of it once and for all!

If you ask me, Epictetus should have started shouting at the top of his lungs. At the very least, it would have made that idiot stop torturing him before his leg broke.

Your neighbour won the lottery and you're jealous

Imagine that your neighbour has just told you that he won a considerable amount of money in the lottery. Or that your boss gave your colleague the promotion you wanted so badly. You're feeling jealous and you're ashamed of it. You think that these sorts of situations shouldn't bother you.

But you're wrong. If you felt no jealousy in these situations, you wouldn't be wise, you'd be a psychopath. The idea that a certain emotional reaction is bad or even morally wrong is totally backwards. Emotions come and go, we can't control them. No emotion is bad in and of itself; what matters is how we handle them.

That's where Cioran hits the nail on the head: 'One must learn not by the example of wise men, but by that of children.'

What do children do? They react immediately to everything that happens in their lives. Children don't censor their emotions. They express them in the first way that comes to mind, then they move on to something else.

If you want to be at peace, don't close yourself off from certain emotions. Explore them.

A meditation on expressing your emotions

Let's try an exercise in two parts. First, take stock of your current emotional state. Don't analyse it. Just try, here and now, to feel what you are experiencing: relaxation, stress, happiness, sadness, whatever it may be. It doesn't matter what. Then, try to come up with a physical way to express your feelings.

If you're having trouble, think about what a child would do. If they're happy, they'll hug your legs or wrap their arms around your neck. If they're sad, they'll bury their head in your shoulder. If they're angry, they'll stomp their feet and scream blue murder. You don't have to be that conspicuous with your expression, of course. Maybe just make a subtle gesture with your arm or your hand.

Allow yourself to experience your own emotional reactions more deeply and to embody them physically. You will feel incredibly liberated. You will discover that you don't have to be stoic or disconnected from your emotions in order to be happy.

'WATER IS TAUGHT
BY THIRST'
EMILY DICKINSON

Knowledge alone is not enough

I can learn a lot about water through pure knowledge but I can't learn its essence. Only experience can teach me the essence of something.

Well, not always. Experience can also lead me astray. For example, I could be absolutely convinced that the person next to me is lying, since I have learned from experience what it feels like to be lied to. But I could still be wrong. Discrimination in its many forms shows us just how often we fall victim to prejudice.

Have you ever truly desired something?

So, how can I learn the essence of something? Listen to Miss Dickinson. She tells us that we cannot learn about water simply by immersing our hands in it but rather by experiencing thirst.

Have you ever really desired something? Then you know that already! The intensity of true desire pushes us to open ourselves up completely to what we are seeking. In that sense, desire is a great teacher.

Today, there is a lot of propaganda which claims that, in order to be happy, we must possess everything that we desire. That we must do everything we dream of doing in order to be satisfied. This is wrong. Instead, it can make us unhappy, as our desire no longer has free rein and we miss out on what it can teach us.

Emily Dickinson, a young woman who lived as a recluse in Massachusetts in the 19th century and who wrote one of the most important collections of poetry in history, alludes to the forgotten intuition of Ancient Greek philosophy with these words. Eros, the god of desire, is the son of Penia, the goddess of poverty and need, and Porus, the god of abundance. Because of his mother, Eros is thin, he wears no shoes and he sleeps under the stars. But thanks to his father, he is persevering, curious and always searching for beauty and good.

What a profound metaphor for desire: to desire is to discover what I lack most deeply and to set out to find it.

For Plato, this is the definition of philosophy itself: not to look for cheap wisdom that is sold by the pound, but to let yourself be seized by your most ardent desire. To set yourself in motion.

A meditation on discovering our true desire

How do we recognise this desire that can awaken us and teach us what we lack most of all?

The difficulty lies in overcoming our tendency to invent new desires for ourselves. What's important is to take the time to listen to what is really calling us. What am I thirsty for? What is missing inside me, preventing me from becoming more completely the person I am meant to be?

Our true desires rise from the deepest parts of ourselves. All we have to do is learn to listen to their call.

I am constantly struck by how most social, political and religious discourse encourages us to extinguish our inner desires. We're supposed to be calm, efficient and submissive to the outside world. It's terrible! After all, the only thing that can make us feel truly alive is that philosophical desire burning within. Only desire can open all of the doors for us.

Without it, without such passion, nothing great could ever be accomplished.

'I DON'T DISGUISE MYSELF
LIKE THOSE WHO WISH
TO APPEAR WISE, WALKING
AROUND LIKE MONKEYS
IN ROYAL ROBES OR
DONKEYS WEARING THE
SKIN OF A LION'
ERASMUS

How do you stay true to yourself?

We all take on different roles in different parts of our lives. It's easy to be critical of this, in the name of a so-called 'authenticity' we should be striving for. Thankfully, though, I am not the same person around my elderly mother as I am around my boss or my three-year-old son.

The idea of being authentic is only meaningful in so far as we adapt our authenticity to the different roles we have to play. The problem arises when we take our roles too seriously and we try to persuade others to take us too seriously.

You're arguing with your partner

You are having a relaxing afternoon at home with your partner and then, all of a sudden, you're arguing over something inconsequential. It starts to get heated. The more you try to prove you're right, the worse you make the situation. Your relationship is no longer important – the bond you shared just a few minutes ago has vanished. All that matters

is winning. You bury yourself in your opinions and princi-
ples. It's clear that the conversation is souring quickly. This
isn't the way you wanted to spend your afternoon.

What should you do?

Stop pretending you're the wise one, or a lion who can
never be wrong. Instead you must accept that you are a
simple monkey, a stubborn donkey, just like everyone else.
Some people are willing to recognise this; others will deny
it to the bitter end.

Nothing good comes of when we act wise and all-knowing,
when we believe our opinion to be above everyone else's and
refuse to consider that we might be wrong. The example I
chose to illustrate this was a quarrel between partners. But
Erasmus wrote these words in response to the terrible wars
that ravaged Europe in his day. In the 16th century, religious conflicts were ferocious. Each side was unwavering in
the view that they were right and their enemies wrong, and
they were prepared to kill to defend their position.

A meditation on letting go of the idealised versions of ourselves

To follow Erasmus's advice, let's practise a short meditation.

Accept the fact that you will never be a perfect mother,
an impeccable father or everyone's favourite colleague.

As soon as you have done so, you will no longer have to uphold the idealised version of yourself that you feel the need to live up to. In your daily life you may have a job title, a role or a set of responsibilities. Don't allow your sense of self to be too strongly tied to any one of these – it will make you rigid.

A friend of mine was once assigned a teaching role at a challenging high school. He was worried about doing a good job. Before the first day of classes, one of the more experienced teachers gave him some advice: 'No matter what you do, you can't manage it all.' Later, my friend told me that he found this remark very liberating.

Erasmus's sentiment is not intended to be despairing or cynical. Quite the opposite. When we stop thinking of ourselves as superhumans who must always succeed, we can finally give ourselves a break. We are freer, more courageous and better able to give the best of ourselves. It's wonderful: drop the mask!

'I WALK TO FIND OUT
WHERE I AM GOING'
*JOHANN WOLFGANG
VON GOETHE*

Stop trying to plan everything in advance

You need to go on a trip, sell your car, bake a cake . . .

You think that you need to plan each step along the way as carefully as possible, in order to be certain that you'll achieve your desired outcome. Before you even begin, you want to anticipate everything you have to do, how it should be done, every problem you could possibly face, and how each one could be handled.

This thinking is certainly appropriate in some situations.

But when it comes to the essence of being human, it's the worst possible approach.

You have an important meeting at work

Let's put this into context. Imagine you have to present your latest project to the board at work this week. Or perhaps you have a job interview or an exam coming up.

You could prepare for it meticulously by writing down and memorising what you're going to say, imagining potential questions and how you'll answer them, and so on. When the time comes for your presentation, it might go perfectly smoothly. But it might also go totally wrong and all of your preparation will prove useless.

You see, you forgot the most important thing: getting to know your audience. Understanding their needs and desires. You forgot how to go about forming a genuine relationship.

First, you must be open to the unpredictable: the questions and comments you couldn't have imagined while you prepared. Be ready to be disconcerted. Only then can a real interpersonal interaction take place. When we tease the class swot, we don't tease them for being wrong but for always being right. They never seem to speak from the heart. When I started speaking at conferences, a friend of mine gave me an invaluable piece of advice: 'Prepare what you want to say as meticulously as possible. Then, once you're at the podium, throw away your notes. Just go down whichever path the audience takes you . . .'

What Goethe, who was a novelist and a poet, as well as a physicist and a politician, wanted us to understand is much more radical than what I'm proposing. Keeping an open mind as I go isn't enough, I must also appreciate that the real meaning of what I am doing will only become apparent when I fully engage with it. If I choose a certain career then little by little, as I gain experience, I will discover what it can teach me. If I decide to write a book, I'll only understand what it means to me by losing myself in writing it. When I'm solely focused on the end goal of my work, the path I take to get there becomes tedious. I only care about reaching the end and arriving at my destination. What a shame! With such a singular focus on the endpoint, I miss out on everything I could learn along the way.

The point of travelling somewhere is the journey itself. That's why Rabbi Naham said, 'Don't ever ask somebody how to get where you're going, because then you might not get lost on the way.'

A meditation on journeys

The next time you decide to go for a walk, experiment a little. First, think about nothing but the destination of your walk. Try to see nothing but the end.

Then, let the end fade into the background and become more attentive to your surroundings as you walk. Let yourself be surprised. Let yourself get lost. This approach will make you much happier.

'WAR IS THE FATHER
OF ALL'
HERACLITUS

Don't give up

Football plays a significant role in our society. At a game, we watch as two teams fight tooth and nail for victory. A fair fight takes place when everyone is playing to the best of their ability. It's a magnificent, exalting experience.

Yet this quote from Heraclitus is disturbing. 'War is the father of all.' Do we really need to fight about everything? Isn't that a rather violent and aggressive idea?

If that's what you're thinking, the problem is that you're confusing combat with violence, even though the two are very different.

Luckily, in football matches, the object of the game is not to eliminate the opposing team. And, luckily for spectators, players never choose to be 'zen' and give up the fight.

You have to write a difficult email

What battles do you have to fight today? Do you have to

force your kids to eat their vegetables? Plan a meeting? Tackle a disagreement with your partner?

You don't know how to go about it and you're annoyed.

I suggest you change your approach and really throw yourself into battle. You'll see, it will change everything. I'm not saying you should fight against something or someone with the goal of destroying whatever stands in your way. No, the battle is to better understand what you need to do or say to fix the situation. Not everything is always as easy as it appears; sometimes you must backtrack or get a little lost in order to find your way.

War is the father of all because, in conflict, everything can appear, can unfold.

Nothing comes without a fight.

For me, this is one of the most captivating legacies of antiquity because it gives us a clear direction. We want things to simply happen, without having to struggle for them. But that's naïve. We think of combat as negative, difficult and tiring. But any task, any project, any creation only exists to the extent that the forces behind it, latent at first, come to light.

You are drafting a note, a contract or an email. You must structure each sentence carefully and choose each word precisely; you must reread it several times to make sure you're conveying exactly the message you intend.

If you forgo this tension, this battle with language, you would forgo the opportunity to say exactly what you mean. This is why the more we tell people they should be calm and detached, the more we teach them powerlessness.

We are happy when we engage in invigorating, creative combat – and succeed.

A meditation on finding the strength for battle

How do you come up with the strength to fight? You need to identify your deepest desire. Let me ask you again: what battles do you have to fight today?

Take a few moments to think about what you are battling for – what you're trying to do, to show and to create through this combat. Soon enough, it will become a passionate fight.

Rather than thinking of battles as exhausting and pointless struggles, try to remember their deeper meaning. Try to be like a great footballer, with fire in your belly. Be full of energy. Be creative. Be passionate.

'THERE IS UNDOUBTEDLY
LITTLE THAT IS SACRED
ABOUT MAN, BUT HIS
HUMANITY SHOULD BE
SACRED TO HIM'
IMMANUEL KANT

Embrace your humanity

Kant starts with a fact: 'There is undoubtedly little that is sacred about man.'

We prove this point every day. We humans have our limits and our imperfections. We sometimes make mistakes and act foolishly. It's only fair to recognise this. However, Kant goes on to say that our own humanity should be sacred to each of us.

What might Kant mean?

Well, let's be careful not to reduce this to some abstract, intellectual idea. Kant is challenging us, inviting us to put our finger on the enigma of our existence. Because what is our humanity? Is it our soul? Is it our reason? Perhaps there is no word that can describe this elusive spark that is within us.

But that doesn't matter. This quote from Kant has had a considerable impact on the history of the West. The idea behind it is at the heart of the Enlightenment, and the notion that all human beings deserve equal rights under the law simply by virtue of the fact that they are human beings.

People keep walking all over you

Some time ago, one of my friends made a mistake at work and his boss reprimanded him aggressively and humiliatingly in public. My friend became totally consumed by the fact that he had allowed himself to commit such an error. And it's true, he did make a mistake. Recognising our mistakes requires honesty, which allows us to move on from them.

However, even if you do make a mistake, you don't deserve to be punished or, even worse, to punish yourself for it. My friend is still a human being. We are all human beings, despite our errors. Strangely, we tend to forget this.

We have a duty to respect our own humanity each and every day.

A meditation on knowing your true self

Imagine that you have made a mistake, behaved badly in an important meeting or failed to complete a simple task. Let's work through it.

Firstly, and quite simply, you must recognise your error. Then, remembering Kant, try to realise that your error does not alter your humanity in the slightest. You have certain unalienable characteristics that constitute your personality: you are a man or a woman of a certain age, with certain tastes, with certain faults and certain skills. Take some time to recognise each of your own unique characteristics. You have done certain things that you are proud of and other things that you regret. Again, try to feel these memories and let them sit with you. You see, none of these attributes can even begin to describe the most fundamental element of your being, that elusive sparkle, the notion of your humanity.

Recognise it. Respect it. It deserves your respect. In fact, your humanity obliges you to respect it. You must respect your humanity not because you are (or are not) rich, kind and attractive; you must respect it simply because you are a human being.

How comforting is that?

'MORALITY IS THE
MOST DARING ACT OF
NARCISSISM'
LOU ANDREAS-SALOMÉ

Reject conformism

Lou Andreas-Salomé, one of the 20th century's most extraordinary thinkers, led a truly remarkable life. At twenty-one years old she met the philosopher Nietzsche, who fell madly in love with her. At thirty-seven, she began a love affair with Rainer Maria Rilke, a great poet, fourteen years her junior. Then, at fifty, in 1911, she developed a close friendship with Sigmund Freud, the father of psychoanalysis.

It is certainly thanks to her interactions with these three figures of Western thought that Andreas-Salomé understood that what humanity was lacking, more than anything else, was sufficient self-regard, or narcissism. This lack of narcissism made people weak and vulnerable to all forms of manipulation.

The situation is no different today. We are blind to it, however, because the term narcissist has come to represent an incontrovertible fault: that of being egocentric, vain and able to think only of oneself. But how has the name of the first flower of spring come to mean something so perverse? It's even more confusing because, throughout the history of Western thought, the character Narcissus has never symbolised someone in love with himself to the point of causing his own death.

Instead, Narcissus symbolises the blossoming of life, that which gives us the power to say 'no' to barbarism and lies. To reject conformism.

You are facing an unjust situation

Allow me to set the scene. At work this morning, one of your managers starts berating the young intern loudly and inappropriately. Your feet are frozen to the floor. Your manager is terrorising the poor young woman and visibly abusing his power. The intern's cheeks get redder and redder. Then she bursts into tears. Some of your co-workers are *laughing*! You don't know what to do. Should you intervene? Say nothing? You're hesitating . . .

In these moments, you must remember Narcissus. You have to find yourself again. By trusting what you think and what you see, you have the power to say 'no' and intervene. Those who resist the status quo must have sufficient faith and trust in themselves to step outside their immediate comfort zone and overcome the temptation to stay quiet.

Lou Andreas-Salomé is right: 'Morality is the most daring act of narcissism.' Being told to kill the narcissism within us, to lose confidence in our own abilities and accept our subsequent guilt, leads to immorality, violence and hatred.

A meditation on being narcissistic

Being narcissistic is not as difficult as you might think. To begin, you must meet the person that you are, right here, right now. Open up to yourself with trust and tenderness. Have empathy for yourself. Reconnect with the vitality inside you, with the forces and passions within you that help you to grow, to be heard and to develop.

By doing so, you are already saying 'yes' to the person that you are – just like you would say it to a child who was suffering. Simply. Without discussion. Without a fuss. You take the child into your arms and you invite them to grow, to take off into the world like a bird into the sky.

'PERHAPS ALL THE
DRAGONS IN OUR LIVES
ARE PRINCESSES, WHO
ARE WAITING TO SEE US
ACT WITH BEAUTY AND
COURAGE'
RAINER MARIA RILKE

Reconnect with your life force

I'm sure you're familiar with stories of knights battling fierce dragons. In Christian tradition, the valiant fighter is most often Saint George. But, of course, knights and dragons can be found everywhere in world mythology. In Greece, Apollo kills the formidable Python. In Egypt, Horus slays the great serpent Apophis with a lance. And the young hero of Wagner's tetralogy, Siegfried, defeats the dragon guarding the fabulous treasure. So, what does this strange animal symbolise?

Well, for one, it represents the underworld, the hidden, swampy place that must be overcome in order to regain our humanity. But the animal isn't always put to death – sometimes the hero tames it. We then see the dragon tied up by a ribbon held by a young girl – she symbolises innocence and the most original kind of knowledge: knowledge of the soul. The child understands that the dragon, beast of antiquity, should not be destroyed but rather understood. The underworld within each of us, then, even though it scares us, should not be eliminated to achieve clarity; it should simply be tamed. After all, darkness contains vitality, life's force. It would be a shame to deprive ourselves of it.

Rilke, visionary poet that he was, proposes a breathtaking interpretation of this myth.

You have been betrayed, harassed or scorned

Imagine that you have recently experienced a moment of profound suffering. You have been betrayed, harassed or scorned by someone you love. What should you do?

Option one: confront the problem directly, with the risk that the ensuing fallout will destroy everything, even you.

Option two: avoid the problem at all costs. Look the other way. Or, to use an expression I am not very fond of, 'let it go'.

A great number of philosophies propose one or the other of these approaches. Rilke offers us a new possibility: allow the hurt to heal and transform into something else.

A meditation on mustering your courage

Okay, but how? You must become intimate with your pain. You must get to know it. You must meet the dragon face to face. This requires courage. It's helpful to remember that the princess within you, your innocence and goodwill, is there to help. The princess within you will get up close to your pain and consider it thoughtfully. She will help you to discover that, if you acknowledge the pain, your injury will heal and become something that helps you. That right there is the true meaning of meditation: relating to and considering the difficulties and hardships of life in a radically different way.

In life, we hear about plenty of recipes and quick fixes that can solve all of our problems. But that's just it: no problems means no dragon. No dragon means no princess. No princess means we have nobody to act with courage and beauty for. Without problems, we are deprived of our ability to solve them and therefore of the most meaningful aspects of life.

'THERE IS NOTHING ON
THIS EARTH THAT WE
SHOULD LOOK DOWN ON
WITH CONDESCENSION'
OLGA SEDAKOVA

Learn to speak to one another

If I look down on you, you most likely won't appreciate it very much. You may even be hurt by it. Why is that? Because someone looking down on you from above has no chance of actually getting to know who they are looking at. The depths of your being, your individuality and richness, will be overlooked.

Countless people are treated with condescension on a daily basis. And the effect it has on them is worse than we tend to acknowledge.

Don't be dismissive

If we want to make a habit of not looking down on people, we have to train ourselves not to look down on anything. Even insignificant objects deserve our careful consideration. Take an apple, for example. Let's try not just to glance at it in passing but to really see it. Apples are special to me because, once upon a time, a very wise guide, a painter, taught me how to look at them properly. It was Paul Cézanne. Throughout his life, Cézanne painted apples in a way that nobody had ever painted them before. Not only did he faithfully depict their countless shapes and sizes, but more fundamentally, he approached each apple that he looked at as if he had never seen an apple before. He looked at them with careful attention, deep affection and great patience. I believe modern art was born the moment Cézanne discovered that an apple is not just a piece of fruit but an opportunity to have a profoundly human experience.

Art critic Meyer Schapiro was so struck by Cézanne's work that he claimed apples were Cézanne's equivalent of the famed nude models in classical paintings. Cézanne looked at apples with the same care that Corrège had for a naked woman's body. For centuries, people thought that perfect bodies or even the deeper questions of existence were interesting, yet apples were not. But perhaps they were wrong. By really *seeing* something as insignificant as an apple, we can touch on larger truths about life, death and justice. This is modernity's most important lesson: looking at everything without any hierarchy.

It's true, I promise. If I look at an apple with genuine consideration, I will learn to look at people, too – especially the marginalised, the oppressed and all the others who are often overlooked. Because everything will become important.

A meditation on saying hello

Let's do an exercise to be like Cézanne and his apples: try saying hello to everything you encounter today.

Look around you. There's a blanket on the sofa, some empty cups in the sink, an umbrella by the door. Say hello to them. Then, allow yourself to be affected by their presence, to enter into an intimate relationship with them. When I look in this way at the teacup sitting on my desk, I realise that it accompanies my long hours of work with great dignity. That teacup isn't just some indifferent, disposable object – it's my companion.

What about that man over there? How can I look at him without looking down on him? By feeling connected to him.

'COLOUR MOVES THE
DEPTHS OF MAN'S
SENSUALITY'
HENRI MATISSE

How to be more in tune

To really embrace the complexity of this quote, I'd like you to try something. Take a look around you and try to only perceive the colours of what you see.

Usually we don't pay close attention. We look at objects and we identify them – we see a tree with green leaves, we don't just see green. Now, perceive only the green and all of its particularities. Let its intensity wash over you. Let the green awaken your most sensual self. It's not separate from you. Your whole being is affected by its vibrations. This experience engages more of your senses than you would have initially thought.

Remember a time something moved you

Remember the first time something moved you deeply. Was it a play you saw? A song you heard? An encounter you had? Perhaps it's possible to experience this in a broader and more profound way. A lot of the time, being moved can remain a superficial experience. I'm moved when I look at a sunset, or when someone gives me a gift. It's quick and sometimes imperceptible.

Matisse takes us on a transformative exploration. This is because, out of nowhere, his quote undermines the whole philosophical structure that we've existed within for centuries, which has led us astray without us even noticing. Essentially, we are led to believe that colour is incidental. It doesn't matter if the jar is blue or green, what's important is that it is a jar. Our emotions don't matter, what's important is our reasoning self. However, this idea prevents us from enjoying a dimension of ourselves that is so close at hand. It's not a question of whether the colour is pretty or nice. That's not what Matisse is trying to teach us. He wants us to allow the colour to inhabit us, transform us and take us places.

A meditation on choosing a shirt

Next time you're choosing a shirt or a scarf to wear, try to pay attention to its colour. Experience it fully. Let it move you. This is a particular experience: it is not physical and sensory, nor is it cerebral and intellectual. It touches a part of us that we have all neglected.

I can now reveal to you the greatest secret of Matisse's

quote. In letting colour stir and touch the deepest part of our souls, it sets us in motion and allows us to access the purest form of joy. Letting the colour in is letting yourself be filled with life. You have discovered the most direct path to finding the joy of being.

Matisse's words illuminate the deeper meaning of another piece of wisdom I'm trying to defend here – that we shouldn't try to shield ourselves from life's intensity, but to celebrate it instead.

'IF YOU WANT TO BE
ORIGINAL, BE HUMAN.
NOBODY IS ANY MORE'
MAX JACOB

What to do about our struggles

We are quick to judge Nietzsche because he went mad late in life, and Virginia Woolf because she committed suicide; we think Monet painted the *Water Lilies* so abstractly because his eyesight had deteriorated; we think Van Gogh's epilepsy is why many of his works contain such intense colours.

These artists were successful not because, in their different ways, they struggled. The secret, for each of them, is the way they made use of their struggle. Genius is born from the way in which one learns about humanity from one's own personal wounds. We find this hard to accept. For most of us, heroes are men with nothing standing in their way, or women with dream jobs, rushing to catch their next flight, not a hair out of place. At least, that's what we're led to believe. Countless TV shows and so-called experts promote this fantasy – they try to teach us to always be at the top of our game, to always perform, never to be aggressive, never to have troubling or painful thoughts . . .

If we listened, we would feel guilty just for being human.

How to be human when nobody is any more

The poet Max Jacob was right: 'If you want to be original, be human. Nobody is any more.' But how?

Nothing could be simpler. All you have to do is give yourself a break!

I came to understand this over many years of paying attention to how often we are judged, examined and evaluated in order to be selected (for such-and-such project, for such-and-such job). You see, we have become used to living in a state of constantly being judged, which requires us never to voice any qualms, troubles or hesitations.

It's time to give ourselves a break and allow ourselves to be human.

The poet's meditation

Max Jacob suggests the following. 'Meditation,' he writes, 'is not about finding or contemplating abstract thought. The point of meditation is to convince yourself of those things you feel that are elementary, to bring out your fundamental emotions, to cultivate your emotions like an actor, to feel your emotions running through your body, especially in that place right between your stomach and your chest. The solar plexus is where the soul resides.'[1]

1   Max Jacob, *in* Yvon Belaval, *La Rencontre avec Max Jacob*, Paris, Charlot, 1946,

Max Jacob is completely right: if we want to be human, we have to rediscover those parts of ourselves that are more fundamental than all of our accomplishments, our successes and our failures. This takes courage. Encountering the most basic elements of our humanity means discovering that we can be touched, hurt and moved by the world . . . and that's frightening. Often, we believe that moving towards such tender self-knowledge will make us unfit for this world: that we'll become too fragile. So we harden ourselves as quickly as possible, crawl into our shell, suppress our true feelings. But the opposite is true. It's the fear of recognising who we really are that weakens us and leaves us hardened, brutish and false.

p. 124.

'DON'T RUSH TO CORRECT
YOUR FLAWS. WHAT
WOULD YOU PUT IN
THEIR PLACE?'
HENRI MICHAUX

Know how to appreciate yourself

When describing our flaws, we have a tendency to be ashamed and to try to get rid of them as quickly as possible. 'Quick, pass the eraser!' we say, for every little thing we don't like. Of course, this kind of thinking leads us to believe that the wisest man is the one with the best eraser. This aspect of my personality is irritating me, so I'd better erase it. That other trait annoys you too. Grab the eraser!

But what would we become after erasing everything? We would be perfectly innocuous beings, with no depth and not much life, either.

Really though, wouldn't it be a good thing if we could eliminate our flaws once and for all? Not at all, because, as the poet Henri Michaux asks us, what would we put in their place? You see, we don't actually fix any problems with our erasers; we only succeed in hurting ourselves.

'Don't rush to correct your flaws.' You have to get to know them first. Make something out of them. Shapes. Or monsters. Or fairies.

This is the most important lesson we can learn from every artist who has resisted the urge to conform. They know how to find strength and opportunity in their flaws, and how to turn their flaws into assets.

You have flaws. How wonderful! Explore them.

You are stuck in a very long queue

Imagine you're standing in the checkout queue at a shop and it's taking forever. You're getting more and more frustrated that you have to keep waiting. Your reaction bothers you. 'If only I weren't so impatient,' you think. But this thought doesn't make you feel any better. In fact, it only deepens your frustration. 'If I weren't so impatient, I'd be a better person.' What a strange idea!

The most extraordinary human beings I've met certainly had their flaws – they just figured out how to make something out of them. The problem with your flaws is that you don't love them, which makes them burdensome and irritating. If you loved your faults, they would offer you precious gifts. You would discover the marvellous wisdom they have to give.

What can you make out of your flaws?

A meditation on irritation

To find out, let's start by trying to determine what irritates you about yourself. Feel how upsetting it is to have whichever characteristic. Feel how much you would like your impatience, your shyness, that particular fear or that particular annoyance to vanish into thin air. Feel how angry you become when you are confronted by one of those characteristics. You are now certainly more tense than you were before we began this exercise.

So now, let's change our approach. Face your problem as if you were listening to a piece of music: with interest and curiosity. Feel the rhythm and the melody . . . You will discover that your impatience, for example, is constantly inviting you to move forward. It is a shimmering, swirling presence. By meditating in this way, you will make peace with yourself. You will put an end to the war that began long ago between yourself and your flaws. You will watch your flaws take on a new appearance, a new life, as you get to know them.

Pretty soon, you won't even recognise them any more. They will stop harming you. And you will come to treasure them.

'MANY THINGS SHOULD
REMAIN SERIOUS, EVEN
IF SOUL MERCHANTS
WANT TO MAKE LIGHT OF
EVERYTHING'
NELLY SACHS

Know when to smile

Has anyone ever told you to smile when you were sad or anxious? I become uncomfortable when I find myself in that situation. It's as if I should feel bad for feeling the weight of things. Smiles are wonderful when they just appear like a gift, but not when they're used to show that nothing is serious.

Ever since I was a child, I have been scolded for being too serious. I allowed everything to affect me deeply, often too much so. When I was younger, I tried to change, without much success. And then I discovered this quote from Nelly Sachs, the poet who won the Nobel Prize for Literature in 1966, and everything fell into place again.

'Many things should remain serious, even if soul merchants want to make light of everything.' Wanting to make light of everything is actually an act of extreme violence. Making everything seem pleasant prevents us from seeing what is unpleasant, what needs to be transformed, changed or refused. It makes us powerless.

You are going to be a father

One of my friends will soon become a father, which makes him very worried. What's more is that he thinks he should be overcome with joy. Isn't that what everyone says? But all that is putting the cart before the horse. We have to start by recognising that fatherhood is a responsibility that can seem daunting. There is a weight to becoming a parent, to bringing life into the world. Only by accepting it can we find true joy in it. Not by denying it.

The Ancient Greeks knew this very well. They invented tragedy to teach people to forge a sacred relationship with the truth of their existence – to accept the significance and consequences of their actions. This idea can lead to a misunderstanding. The goal is not to find gravity in everything. Wishing to make everything serious or wishing to make light of everything are both the same mistake.

The art of being human consists of precisely weighing each situation, each event, knowing when to make light of what's at hand, and when to take it seriously. Striking the right balance.

A meditation on giving proper weight to your emotions

To learn this art, consider an emotion that you are currently experiencing, or one that you have experienced in the last few days. Take the time to get to know it. In which part of your body do you feel its presence most directly? In your chest? In your belly? In your throat? What if your emotion had a shape, a physical form? What would it look like? If it had a colour, what colour would it be? What sensation do you associate with the emotion you're feeling? Is it a pinching sensation? A squeezing sensation? Heat?

Perhaps now you can name the emotion: is it grief? Loneliness? Tenderness?

By trying this exercise and by exploring the emotion you are experiencing, you are giving it its proper weight and proper consideration. No more, no less.

'EVER TRIED. EVER FAILED.
NO MATTER. TRY AGAIN.
FAIL AGAIN. FAIL BETTER'
SAMUEL BECKETT

The art of failure

Are you afraid of failure? Is it painful to you? If so, this quote from Samuel Beckett was made for you. It completely turns on its head the idea that failure means being at fault.

You would like to learn a new skill

Imagine you would like to learn a new skill: the tango, rowing, or whatever you fancy.

As an example, think of a child learning how to walk. When he falls down again and again, he doesn't become discouraged and decide he will never be able to walk. Quite the opposite. The child must fall down over and over again in order to learn how to get back up and, little by little, he'll learn to walk. If you aren't prepared to fall down sometimes, you shouldn't try to stand. You might as well give up on life! Rejecting the possibility of failure means condemning yourself to powerlessness. Accepting it will allow you to succeed.

But Beckett doesn't tell us simply to accept failure in order to succeed later. He invites us to 'fail better'. Why? Does he want us to confine ourselves to failure and suffering? Not at all. He's calling for exactly the opposite. To 'fail better' means to accept wholeheartedly the profound meaning of failure and discover how to incorporate this into the very essence of your life.

Have you ever seen Proust's marked-up manuscripts? They offer quite a lesson in failure! Onto his edited manuscripts, full of crossed-out words and sentences, Proust would often glue little pieces of paper, which he called 'paperolles' and which allowed him to add a sentence or a paragraph here and there. Proust proves that being a great writer means understanding the art of failing well. Every time Proust picked up his manuscripts, he was constantly thinking about sentences that weren't quite right and passages that could be added or deleted. You see, the point isn't to overcome your failures, but to immerse yourself in them so completely that they transform the project you set out to create.

A meditation on an everyday dilemma

So, let's start with the assumption that you can accept the fact that failure is a part of life. But you have an objection: sometimes failure is painful. Yesterday evening, you had some friends over for dinner and the tart you baked for dessert tasted a little burned. You feel bad.

Let's examine the situation. Your first reaction is anger. It's your oven's fault because it doesn't work properly. It's your kids' fault because they always ask you for something at just the wrong moment. Or perhaps you conclude that you are simply not very good at baking. None of these approaches help.

These days, we put a lot of emphasis on success, but we never learn to work with the fact that sometimes things don't turn out the way we'd like. So, how can we overcome these annoyances? Instead of reacting in anger or despair, recognise that you are hurt, that you feel pain. Already, you're failing better by getting in touch with your own fragility, your own humanity. Can you allow yourself to feel what you are experiencing? Can you accept the fact that sometimes not everything turns out the way you'd like it to?

'INTELLIGENCE IS
CHARACTERISED BY A
NATURAL INABILITY TO
COMPREHEND LIFE'
HENRI BERGSON

How to get meaning back into your life

If anyone but Henri Bergson, one of the great French philosophers, had said these words, we might think they were joking. How can intelligence prevent us from understanding life? It seems unlikely. After all, intelligence is what takes us beyond our primal reflexes and prejudices, and we certainly need more of that in today's world. So, what does Bergson mean?

Let's start by defining intelligence. Intelligence is what creates order out of chaos. It allows us to discover rules and patterns in our world's diverse phenomena. In other words, it allows us to form generalisations. Incredible! Intelligence gives us the capacity to expand our understanding of reality. But here's the problem: by constantly generalising, intelligence eliminates the profundity, the ever-changing nature and richness of our own unique experiences. In other words, intelligence makes us miss out on life.

You are often bored

Do you sometimes get bored? No doubt it's because you are too clever. Yes, you've read that correctly.

Take the following situation. You have a lunch date this weekend at your in-laws'. Before you even step through the door, you know exactly what food they will serve and exactly what you will talk about at the table. The whole meal promises to be dull and painful. Your intelligence is causing you to generalise the experience of lunchtime with your in-laws. You see, once you sit down for lunch, you're not going to taste the tomato salad they made but the idea of a tomato salad. Your intelligence has turned that salad into an abstraction of a salad, not the unique, incomparable one in front of you now, which deserves to be fully savoured.

If you want your life to be more thrilling, you need to put your intelligence to one side and come back to individual sensations: specific perceptions, emotions, feelings . . . It takes a certain effort to go beyond our normal intellectual reflexes to enjoy a rich and unique experience. But it's worth it!

A meditation on freeing yourself from the burden of your intelligence

Here's a short meditation to help you put aside your powerful intellect – which tends to categorise everything in advance.

Now, wherever you are, simply open yourself up to the richness of everything you are experiencing. Perhaps you will notice a detail of your sitting room that you have never observed before, like the design on a lampshade or the carpet in front of you. You have probably looked at that lamp or that carpet every day for years, yet it's the first time in your life that you have considered it with such an open mind.

If you want to be happy, you must trust in the power of a constantly new gaze.

'MAN SHOULD NOT TRY TO DISPEL THE AMBIGUITY OF HIS BEING BUT, ON THE CONTRARY, ACCEPT THE TASK OF REALISING IT'
SIMONE DE BEAUVOIR

Don't erase the grey areas

This quote isn't easy to understand. Let's take our time with it. We call something ambiguous when it has several meanings, several sides, or when it could go in several different directions. In general, we try to avoid such ambivalence. We like everything to have an unequivocal meaning, at the risk of it becoming one-dimensional. We prefer to sacrifice ambiguity for the sake of efficacy.

A great number of political theories and ideologies are based on this notion. They strive to eradicate any kind of opacity. They want to erase all colour, all of the grey areas, in favour of the objectivity of black and white. It's become something of a sport in our era of public relations.

You must make a decision

But is getting rid of ambiguity always a good idea? Let's think about this using an example from everyday life. You have to make a big decision – for example, whether or not to break things off with your partner, move to another part of the country or accept a job offer. You don't know what to do. In fact, what you see as a difficulty is an opportunity. Because, if you are deliberating, it's because you are free. If there was only one option – one potential partner, one apartment, one job – it would be awful. Making choices is one of the richest experiences that life has to offer. The trade-off, however, is that you can never be a hundred per cent certain that the option you choose is the best one available. We often forget that free choice is a dizzying experience.

Simone de Beauvoir was passionate about freedom. That's why she emphasises the danger of our desire to simplify everything. The current idea that we should always be calm, cool and collected, completely in control of every part of our lives, does nothing but deny our freedom. Instead, we must learn to embrace ambiguity, openness and the range of possibilities that life offers.

A meditation on your sense of humour

So, how to do it? Meditating on your sense of humour will help immensely. This means recognising that there's a little bit of Buster Keaton or Charlie Chaplin in all of us, and asking them to help out.

Imagine you've just bought a new pair of shoes. A few days later, you see a different pair in a shop window and a wave of doubt washes over you. You should have bought those shoes instead! In these moments, you have to let your inner Charlie Chaplin evaluate the situation, and show you how to laugh about it.

When you take things too seriously, any ambiguity can be disheartening. But when you turn towards your sense of humour, you can find the funny side of any situation, instead of getting frustrated.

If you consider your situation from several different angles or take a bird's-eye view, everything becomes easier.

'COFFEE IS A LOT MORE
THAN JUST A DRINK; IT'S
SOMETHING HAPPENING
[. . .] IT GIVES YOU TIME'
GERTRUDE STEIN

A little philosophy every day . . .

How does drinking coffee give you time to think? For most of us, 'thinking' for any period of time is usually associated with the lofty, intellectual pursuit of some kind of clarity or knowledge. Life's daily activities are hardly comparable. If they bring us pleasure at all, it is a relatively superficial and uninspiring kind of satisfaction.

Gertrude Stein, the celebrated 20th-century poet and friend of Picasso, thought exactly the opposite. Everyday activities can be profoundly meaningful and can actually help us to transform our entire existence.

Stressed out?

I have a suggestion for you. Drink a cup of coffee. If you don't like coffee, a cup of tea or hot water with lemon will work just as well. The point is simply to take the time to drink your drink. You can change your whole relationship with time by doing something as effortless as that.

You will sit there, with the extraordinary smell of your coffee or tea, preparing your palate for its unique flavour. When you let yourself take the time to really imbibe it, really get the taste of it in all of its richness, you're already taking off, preparing to fly through the substance of time.

In other words, as you sit there enjoying your coffee, you're actually doing something that has nothing to do with the mug in your hands. You're disengaging from the usual worries of daily life. This is what gives you the space to think, the time to consider new ideas.

Even after you've finished your coffee, you still have some time to sit there and think a little longer. The important thing is that when you took that break from everyday life to drink your coffee, in a very simple sense, everything changed. Whatever was stressing you out a few minutes ago is now just a mild annoyance. You are more available, more receptive.

Be careful not to confuse this profound experience with what many people call 'appreciating life's small pleasures'. This is not about enjoying the little things. Drinking coffee is about liberating your own existence from top to bottom.

Before she moved to Paris, Gertrude Stein was one of the most fervent students of William James, the American philosopher who redefined how we understood human consciousness. The life of the mind, James explained, is comparable to that of a bird, often alternating between flying and resting. Human beings can only truly find the joy of being alive when they strike a comfortable balance between these extremes.

When you stop for a moment to drink your coffee, tea or hot water with lemon, you allow yourself to recognise that your mind doesn't always have to race forward at full speed. Instead, it can move like a dancer to ever-changing music: sometimes faster, sometimes slower.

A meditation for the shower

You can perform this exercise during any activity that allows you to take a little break and, therefore, to briefly change your relationship with time. Personally, I like to meditate this way in the shower. While I'm taking my shower, I allow myself to be distracted by how pleasant the hot water feels, and then, for a short while, I'm able to forget my everyday worries. When I get out, I feel a little different on the inside, as if everything had shifted slightly.

What about you? What everyday activities give you time to think?

'WE CANNOT
UNDERSTAND THE PAST
WITHOUT THE PRESENT'
MARC BLOCH

Ask questions

This quote from Marc Bloch, one of the great French philosophers of the first half of the 20th century, is a little confusing because we instinctively believe that history is the study of what has happened in the past.

But there is no objective past, nothing fixed in another time for us to discover. This might be surprising, but Marc Bloch is right. We can only tease out a perspective on history by answering the questions we ask about it. It's useless to try to understand history by memorising names and dates like a shopping list. We won't discover anything unless we enquire into it – which is why being a historian is far more about asking questions than recording facts.

Think back to a turning point in your life

Think about your own life and you'll see exactly what I mean. If you had a tough time in your childhood, for example, you are only able to make sense of it now, as the person you are today. Perhaps something happened that you haven't thought about in years. And then, one day, all of a sudden, you recall that experience in great detail. That's usually not just by chance.

You see, your own history is not at all fixed in time. It's only from your present vantage point that you are able to welcome it, or not, and a particular episode from your life may resurface or stay buried. A past event, which was difficult and painful at the time, might seem worthwhile to you now because it opened doors that you would never have found otherwise.

Being human means understanding that – just like the history of the world – we constantly need to rethink our past.

A meditation on Notre-Dame

Like many of you, I was devastated as I watched Notre-Dame burn down. But why?

If we thought of Notre-Dame as nothing but a structural remnant of the Middle Ages, a monument frozen in time, it would be difficult to understand why so many people, especially those who are not Christian or particularly interested in French heritage, were so upset about the fire.

Let's think like Marc Bloch. What does Notre-Dame mean to us? Not just yesterday, but today?

You don't have to be an architect to realise how excep-
tional the cathedral is. It literally reaches to the heavens. It
invites us all to experience something bigger than ourselves,
something that towers over us in every sense imaginable.
We can experience Notre-Dame and relate to it according
to our individual past, our beliefs and our own unique lives.

But, for each of us, when the great spire fell, it was that
feeling of elevation that we felt collapse.

'NEVER DESPISE A
PERSON'S SENSITIVITY. HIS
SENSITIVITY IS HIS GENIUS'
CHARLES BAUDELAIRE

What if our defining characteristic isn't reason?

We tend to think that our ability to reason is what defines us as human. There is a long tradition behind this belief: that our bodies, being below our heads, are inferior to our brains and so it is our minds that connect us to something larger than ourselves. This belief is why we seek to elevate ourselves – through education – from our imperfect, confused sensitivities to reach for conceptual clarity and higher reasoning.

Baudelaire's quote turns this notion on its head: sensitivity is not an obscure, blind domain but rather a mode of deep understanding, unique and definitive.

You must go to the beach!

You're on holiday and you've planned to spend the whole afternoon at the beach. But is that what you really want?

Last summer, one of my friends realised, to her great surprise, that she didn't actually like the beach that much. She'd never really allowed herself to acknowledge this but had forced herself to go along with her family. It's not always easy to know exactly what you're feeling. Many people don't know what they like and this deprives them of precious knowledge.

Baudelaire invites us to discover something even more radical. Our sensitivities are not only a kind of knowledge but the source of our genius, guiding us in our lives. I didn't choose my profession based solely on my technical skills, but also by considering my feelings and inclinations, what I like and what makes me happy.

This is why I think we are wrong to measure medical students' aptitude based solely on their scientific and mathematical skills. We should also take into account their understanding of what it means to be human, their compassion for people in general and their understanding of pain. Of course, technical skills are important in order to be a good doctor, prerequisites even. But they are not the sole determinant of success. The ability to diagnose, to listen to patients and talk to them are all qualities that are essential in a physician. So, why don't we give them due consideration?

Exploring our sensitivities is hard work. And we are just as handicapped in doing this as we are ignorant of how to approach this task. In school, we are only shown the way in arts classes. For example, in music, you learn what sound is and how it touches you, but this only scratches the surface.

A meditation on sensitivity

Let us learn to work on our sensitivity. You can do this with anything around you – for example, fruit.

Gather some of the fruits that are in season and take a moment to embrace their presence. Try holding one in your hand. Feel it. Then another. Appreciate its colour, the texture of its skin. Perhaps you will discover that you feel like having an apricot but are not tempted by the strawberries. Fantastic. This is a great start. Now, simply pay attention to your relationship with the fruit. Embrace your own sensitivity.

This little exercise will help you to rediscover your own unique genius.

'I MARVEL AT THE
EXISTENCE OF THE WORLD'
LUDWIG WITTGENSTEIN

It is crucial to learn to be astonished

Ludwig Wittgenstein, one of the greatest philosophers of the 20th century, hosted just one public lecture in his life. Its subject was ethics. At the end of the lecture, he addressed his audience in the first person, unlike in the rest of his speech, and confided in them that the very meaning of life, for him, was to marvel at the world's very existence.

His message might be disconcerting, as often we think that philosophy is about abstract thought. But Wittgenstein tells us we're wrong.

Take a moment to look at the sky

From a strictly logical perspective, Wittgenstein's sentence doesn't make much sense. I can be surprised at the fact that my good friend has suddenly decided to move halfway across the world, or I can be surprised at seeing an oversized dog in the lobby of my apartment building. In other words, I can be surprised and marvel at something I wasn't expecting or that should not have taken place. But it seems absurd to marvel at the existence of the world because I cannot imagine what my life would be like if the world, as we know it, did not exist.

Let's do an experiment to explore the difference between these two kinds of wondering. Allow yourself to marvel at the fact that the sky today is clear and blue instead of cloudy. Then, allow yourself to marvel at the fact that the sky exists in the first place. The second experience is not at all the same. When you consider the miracle that is the sky's existence, you set aside your usual way of being, of perceiving and thinking about your surroundings.

Logically speaking, we can only 'marvel' in the strictest sense of the word at the fact that the sky is clear today rather than cloudy. 'Marvelling' at the fact that the sky exists in the first place is borderline nonsense. But Wittgenstein insists that we recognise the value of the second experience. It tells us something profound about the meaning of life, which Wittgenstein calls ethics and which is a personal and intimate experience for each of us.

A meditation on marvelling

Take a moment, right now, and try to marvel at the existence of the world. This exercise might seem daunting and abstract, but in fact it's simple.

The hard part is that you have to really live the experience. Imagine I am describing a fruit that you have never tasted before. The more I talk about it, the less clear it becomes to you. But the fruit that I'm describing is not abstract at all. It's real. If you had one, you could taste it for yourself.

Philosophy is like trying to understand the taste of a fruit you've never eaten. It makes us experience our lives, the good parts and the bad, in a totally different way. This is what we fundamentally misunderstand about philosophy. On the one hand, the philosophy that introduces us to new cognitive experiences often seems abstract and impractical, when in fact it is quite real and can totally alter our day-to-day lives. This philosophy encourages us to shift gears, change our point of view and helps us see the world more clearly. On the other hand, the 'philosophy' that gives us soundbites of wisdom, which purport to be practical, does nothing but blind us, dooming us to repeat our mistakes. It is this brand of philosophy that is abstract, not Wittgenstein's. It has nothing to do with real life. The difference between these two approaches is the capacity to marvel at the world as it is.

The act of marvelling at the world is profoundly philosophical because it alone can transform our entire way of being.

'POETRY IS THE FIRST
MILLIMETRE OF AIR ABOVE
THE EARTH'S SURFACE'
MARINA TSVETAEVA

The inhumanity of numbers

Our reality today tends to be defined almost exclusively by numbers. Schools are measured by their test scores, unemployment is represented by a curve. Bit by bit, life is obscured by statistics. There is a new form of fanaticism, which, like all fanaticisms, imposes a single, set perspective on reality. This perspective crushes us and, if we subscribe to it, we risk becoming the living dead – nothing more than a data set.

In truth, real life is what we do every day: take a shower, make dinner, speak with so-and-so, respond to such-and-such email, look both ways before crossing the street . . . None of this has anything to do with numbers, but these tasks do demand presence.

We have to take it one step further than that. We need to make an effort to open ourselves up to the present and let it be.

I remember the first time I visited Brittany, France's most picturesque province, as a young man. To my great surprise, I didn't really see anything. Sure, I saw the sea, the cliffs, the beautiful blue sky and so on. It was all very pretty. But being there gave me the strange feeling of being trapped inside a postcard. It took me several days to no longer view the landscape as a photograph and to really be moved with all my being.

You can't get down to work

So, how can I learn to see something beyond how it is conventionally viewed, like in postcards?

It takes hard work – that's the secret to reaching tangible results and feeling like we're in touch with reality. That might be tricky to get our heads around, as we have this idea that work has to be painful, even punishing. We think that we have to sacrifice ourselves to our work, so that maybe, at some distant point in the future, we might be able to reap the rewards. But that isn't work that helps us to open up to the world around us. Useful work is the kind that makes everything grow.

Working to play a piece of music flawlessly, working to cultivate your garden and see your flowers bloom, working to help your children grow – *that*'s the kind of work that brings us closer to reality and happiness. In each of these examples, our inner passion pushes us to move forward, to get in touch more completely with reality and allow reality, in turn, to respond to us.

A meditation on what allows us to breathe

In this respect, for Marina Tsvetaeva, all work is related to poetry, as it helps us to discover the secret of things. I remember, as a child, watching my grandfather, who was a tailor, at work. I was absolutely transfixed. It seemed to me like he entered into the realm of the fabrics he touched – he handled them with such graceful dexterity. It was my first experience of poetry.

What about you? What allows you to breathe?

A common misunderstanding is that poetry consists of appreciating the small things, the present moment. But that's a naïve and limiting view and won't allow you to breathe. We are able to breathe when we're no longer stuck in the mundane, habitual, inflexible reality that our obsession with numbers forces on us. Without poetry, the present moment is burdensome, monotonous and tedious.

'TAKE CARE OF YOURSELF'
SOCRATES

Why you need to think about your own needs

This quote sums up Socratic thinking and introduces us to all of Western philosophy. Socrates often went to public squares to meet people and to ask them about their lives. For example, he met a young man from a good family, Alcibiades, who said that he wanted a fulfilling job, to become a respectable man and to become more powerful.

'All right,' said Socrates, 'that is all understandable, but are you taking care of yourself?' Alcibiades did not understand the meaning of this question at all. And with good reason: it is an unexpected question. Society asks a lot of us, sometimes to the point of self-sacrifice, and here is a man instructing us to take care of ourselves! The Athenians were so furious that they sentenced Socrates to death. For them, the goal of education was to produce efficient workers, ready to enter the job market, not free men who thought for themselves.

Any semblance to our current situation is no coincidence.

You are deeply troubled

'Take care of yourself.' This proposition has unfortunately inspired two misinterpretations, which have completely deprived it of its original meaning.

The first is thinking that taking care of yourself means cutting yourself off from the rest of the world and taking refuge in what the Stoics call our 'inner fortress'. What a misinterpretation! Socrates' approach is not one of ascetic withdrawal but of civic involvement. He invites us to engage with the world around us, not to flee from it.

The second misinterpretation is that the act of taking care of oneself requires mastery over one's urges and emotions. But the goal of taking care of oneself is not mastery but letting go. Socrates does not seek to lead us to the security of wisdom and serenity but to question our position in existence.

If Socrates were to come and talk to you, you would certainly be far from serene and probably very uncomfortable. Are you already feeling uncomfortable?

Wonderful! That's the best way to enter into a philosophic experience. But what to do with this feeling of discomfort, since the goal is not to dispose of it in order to find inner peace?

A Socratic meditation

To find out, we must engage in Socratic meditation. Plato tells us that Socrates often stood completely still, without moving. Once, he even stayed standing from one dawn to the next, to the astonishment of everyone around him. What was he doing?

When Socrates was in a difficult situation, he stopped and put himself in the centre of his trouble, even just for a moment. Without doing anything. Without looking for a solution.

You don't have to stand still for long but put yourself back into this state of not-knowing. Enter this most fundamental of positions, of ideologies, of identities. Then everything, truly everything, can change.

To think philosophically is not to have all the answers, or even to have in-depth knowledge, but to be seized by the overwhelming need to think about what matters most to you, here and now.

'THE CAPACITY TO
PAY ATTENTION [. . .]
IS A MIRACLE'
SIMONE WEIL

Overcoming our technology addiction

The necessity of paying attention is particularly acute these days when entire industries are based on robbing us of our capacity for concentration. Most recent surveys show that the average attention span is getting shorter and shorter – at the moment, it is nine or ten seconds. After that, our brains tend to wander. We need new stimulus, a new signal, alert or activity. We hoped that the digital age would expand our knowledge and relationship skills, but instead it is restricting them.

A 2017 study from the American Psychological Association showed that people spend an average of 2.8 seconds in front of a painting while visiting a museum. It is highly improbable that we can truly appreciate a work of art in that short span of time.

Take care to listen actively

Try to be attentive the next time you're having a conver-sation with someone. And no, it isn't as easy as it sounds.

We don't know how to do this well. We have a tendency to tense up and clench our jaws, to think that we need to really work to pay attention. But this only makes us agitated. What is truly important, on the contrary, is that we make ourselves available.

This implies that we accept a degree of uncertainty. In order to listen properly to what others have to say, we must accept that we do not know in advance what they're going to tell us. Since this can be uncomfortable, we look frantically for the nearest exit. And our current technology uses neuroscience to exploit this. Our devices constantly demand our attention, relieving us of this feeling of uncertainty. But this is a false relief. Little by little, technology cuts us off from our humanity, from what we feel, from what we want. We are robbed of our selves.

It's a strange paradox: the more I look at my phone screen, checking some app or another, the more I isolate and empty myself. And vice versa. The more I listen to others, accepting that I cannot know in advance what they will say, the more I enter into a profound and real relationship with them, and the more I discover myself.

A meditation on a tree

So, what can you do? Learn to strengthen your attention with micro-mediations – on a tree, for example. Begin by looking at a tree and practise being astonished by its presence. From there, explore the singularity of its being – what makes it special? Perhaps it has a particular shape, or perhaps its leaves have a certain way of catching the light? What about its colours? Notice how, bit by bit, the centre of this situation has shifted from you to the tree. It is a comforting experience to be able to welcome this tree, just as you would welcome a person – greeting them, listening to them.

Our capacity to pay attention is truly a miracle, available to everyone, at any given moment.

'IT BEGAN TO DAWN UPON MODERN MAN THAT HE HAD COME TO LIVE IN A WORLD IN WHICH HIS MIND AND HIS TRADITION OF THOUGHT WERE NOT EVEN CAPABLE OF ASKING ADEQUATE, MEANINGFUL QUESTIONS'
HANNAH ARENDT

When the tyranny of profitability threatens you

Hannah Arendt invites us to break free of a common misconception: that human beings across time and space are all the same. At first glance, this hypothesis seems reasonable. But actually, thinking that way keeps us from recognising our own particular suffering. What is specific to our time that we are not aware of?

Our suffering arises from the fact that we only consider real that which we can account for, manage or enter into a spreadsheet. By such thinking, a tree is a carbon dioxide reservoir, which with proper management can yield the best output. Thus, overly diverse forests are destroyed to make room for the most optimal, profitable tree varieties. And what is an animal? A source of calories. And death camps disguised as slaughterhouses allow us to maximise production. What about human beings? They are resources that must be managed in order to draw maximum profit.

This was not the prevalent line of thinking during the Middle Ages. At that time, everything real was created by God. In line with this philosophy, Saint Francis often spoke of the trees and the birds as his brothers. But now, everything is different.

You're on the verge of burnout

You are exhausted. You feel like you're about to burn out.

You are told that you need to better manage your stress. But this is a good example of a mistaken analysis – it entirely misses the point of the situation. The problem does not stem from your stress management. It comes from the fact that you are being used by people who only want to get maximum profit from you, and who disregard who you are in the process.

And you've reached breaking point. Bear in mind that the same kind of manager is found everywhere, be it in a hospital, a large insurance company or an airline. This goes to show that the specifics of each job are, for them, meaningless.

A meditation on taking a walk

We are already deeply impacted by this obsession with profitability and results. For example, the simple act of going for a walk. Thanks to a health app, you can keep track of how many steps you take, your heart rate and the calories you've burned, and as a result you're constantly trying to keep up and do better. The simple pleasure of taking the time just to exist, to do something, to accomplish something, disappears.

Hannah Arendt is right: wisdom that doesn't take into account our history, far from helping us, can only destroy us, which is exactly what is happening right now. And that's why we need philosophy more than ever: to teach us to ask these simple questions.

'I DISPATCH A POT OF JAM IN ORDER TO GET RID OF A BITTER EXPERIENCE'
FRIEDRICH NIETZSCHE

How to avoid confrontation

Nietzsche proposes that we create a diversion. When faced with a difficult situation, perhaps an aggressive one, we should avoid confrontation at all costs. Why? Because, while we think we are defending ourselves, we remain prisoners of our opponent. When someone insults you or yells at you, returning their insult is the best way to fall into their trap. If we want to rise above the situation, we must adopt a much more subtle strategy.

You're angry with someone who has wronged you

Here's an example: someone you considered a friend has insulted you behind your back and betrayed you. How do you avoid falling into a cycle of retaliation? How do you rise above the anger that naturally envelops you? For Nietzsche, the important thing is not to fall into that trap.

But how? You don't want to let yourself get walked over either. Free yourself from the idea that your only options are fighting or giving in. Nietzsche invites us to be much more creative. He invites us to send a pot of jam, not to the person who has hurt us – that would just be silly – but to temper the bitterness of the situation. A little jam to sweeten what you're caught up in, what you're imprisoned by. The point is to liberate yourself.

There are two ways of responding. Either you contradict your opponent: they say black, you say white, but this just means playing a game that they started. Or you can question the opposition: why does everything have to be black or white? Maybe it's more nuanced than that . . .

A meditation on good intentions

Think about a frustrating or irritating situation that made you tense. You want to react, to respond to the situation, to get out of there – even at the risk of being aggressive. Now try to feel, despite your frustration or irritation, something that makes you really happy. This could be a fond memory or a moment in which you felt content.

This is a way of passing from resentment to feeling. What is resentment, really? A reaction that limits us, boxes us in and alienates us from life. What about feeling? It's everything that gives life meaning and colour: all that delights and opens us to the world.

Perhaps now you understand that Nietzsche is not giving us a little tip on how to behave better, but much more importantly, he is inviting us to understand our existence in a different light; to understand that to exist is to be in harmony with life and to say 'yes' to it, rather than blaming it.

Philosophy has much to teach us, by inviting us to partake in such deep experiences.

'LANGUAGE CAN BE A TRUE BATTLEFIELD, A PLACE OF OPPRESSION, BUT ALSO OF RESISTANCE'
TONI MORRISON

When words destroy

This quote from Toni Morrison, one of America's greatest authors, is taken from a conversation between the author and the French sociologist Pierre Bourdieu. With it, Morrison exposes the way in which stereotypes can play a powerful role in the alienation of others, particularly that of black people.

What really strikes me about this quote is how it helps us to understand an author's responsibility. The author's responsibility is not primarily, as one might think, in their political commitments, or the stories that they tell but, more fundamentally still, in their way of returning to words their power of resistance. And primarily, their power to resist stereotypes.

It was only some years later, while reading Victor Klemperer, that I understood that Morrison was right: language can be a form of oppression. Victor Klemperer was a German linguist, who was forced to live in secrecy once Hitler rose to power. He had the surprising idea of keeping a diary in which he detailed just how the

Nazis were transforming everyday language. To this effect, Klemperer notes: 'Words can be like tiny doses of arsenic: you swallow them carelessly, nothing seems to happen, and then, after a while, the poison suddenly sets in.' This is exactly what Toni Morrison wants us to see: how words can dehumanise those who they are describing.

In Nazi Germany, human beings were referred to as 'elements', being detained in 'concentration camps', to be eventually 'liquidated'.

What about black people? How have they been deprived of their full existence? How have they been confined to stereotypes?

Toni Morrison points out that black people have long been associated in literature with terms like 'savage', 'innocent', 'wise', yet also 'brutal'. The fact that these adjectives directly contradict one another isn't the point. They were not used to better understand, but rather to deprive people of their singularity through labelling. Toni Morrison thus took upon herself the responsibility of restoring English at various levels, incorporating street vernacular and colloquial language, lyrical and biblical language, into her contemporary register, in an effort to restore dignity to black Americans, and give them back their own voices. For Morrison, this was a way to allow black Americans to escape the oppression inflicted upon them.

Managing your stress

Today's language prevents us from confronting the violence of our everyday lives in new ways. Take, for example, the expression 'to manage your stress', which seems totally innocent at first glance. It is precisely because it is so seemingly banal that it is so problematic. This expression reduces humans to something like stock, which can be regulated with better accounting methods. Only your bank account should be 'managed', certainly not your stress, your emotions or your feelings! You should encounter these things, listen to them or even soothe them.

Human beings suffer not because we haven't managed our stress, but rather because we feel the need to manage it and are, as a result, cut off from our humanity.

When I point out these problems, some might say I'm just playing with words. But no. Words can manipulate us and keep us from recognising the violence we suffer, which dehumanises us. I am not calling for an academic respect for language. After all, it's poets and authors who play with language and who often best manage to put words to our experience, what we are living. And Toni Morrison strikes me as a prime example of this.

A meditation on stress

What do you call your stress?

What does this word mean to you? How do you relate to it? Where do you experience it?

Try now to determine what you feel when I tell you to manage it. And what if, on the other hand, I ask you simply to feel it, to soothe it . . .

'IT TOOK MANY YEARS
OF VOMITING UP ALL THE
FILTH I'D BEEN TAUGHT
ABOUT MYSELF, AND HALF-
BELIEVED, BEFORE I WAS
ABLE TO WALK ON THE
EARTH AS THOUGH I HAD
A RIGHT TO BE HERE'
JAMES BALDWIN

Becoming strong

This quote illustrates James Baldwin's bitter experience in analysing and overcoming his suffering as a black man in the US during the 1940s and 1950s.

But his analysis is relevant to us all. The simple fact of not being like other people – of not being the right ethnicity or sexual orientation, of being disabled, or a woman in a man's world, of having tastes or aspirations that don't fit with conventional societal norms – can make us feel like there's something wrong with us. But this suffering is political, not psychological.

It's not easy for us to understand this because we usually understand politics in abstract terms: as a simple opposition between ideas and doctrines. But, in reality, politics often manifests itself in our very flesh. It leaves us battered and scarred as it convinces us to believe in its lies.

Ask yourself: what views of yourself have you internalised?

Do you believe other people's opinions of you to be true? Who has wounded you? Who has put you in a box and judged you? The problem with identifying this is that we're often not even aware of it happening in the first place. And for good reason. We human beings are immensely fragile. Too often, we believe that we are somehow deserving of the violence we suffer.

A child who has been abused by their parents will believe, against all logic, contrary to all of the facts, that they are responsible for the evil they have endured. A child who is abandoned by their mother, for example, will think that it is their fault, that they are not worthy of her love.

And this often follows us into adulthood. Our inner child exhausts itself by desperately trying to be perfect, or sacrificing itself for others in the hope that it will finally be accepted, loved and recognised. But these efforts are in vain and only take us further from what we want.

A meditation on reclaiming our dignity

How do we reclaim our dignity when it has been stolen from us? Like Baldwin, we must vomit up the filth we have ingested.

What a noble act! When we are ill, when we have eaten something bad, we have to vomit it up, to purge our stomach. And that's how we recover our health. We have to do the same with ideological poison. We have to use the most extraordinary of meditations: the meditation of noble vomiting.

It's very simple. Most importantly, don't try to justify yourself, to explain yourself or defend yourself. Free yourself from the filth. Accept that you won't assimilate what is impossible to assimilate. You don't have to feel that you are not enough. You don't have to feel guilty. Banish those feelings. Ignore any view of you that oppresses you.

While you are not responsible for the violence you endure, it is your duty to free yourself from it.

'IF YOU'RE ALWAYS TRYING
TO BE NORMAL, YOU
WILL NEVER KNOW HOW
AMAZING YOU CAN BE'
MAYA ANGELOU

Finding the courage to be yourself

Maya Angelou was an important moral figure in American artistic and political life. In 1993, at the request of President Bill Clinton, she read one of her poems at his inauguration.

It was a powerful and historic moment – to see a black woman, born into great poverty and having faced so many challenges in her life, rising to speak out boldly, with strength and courage, in front of all of America. She demonstrated the power of poetry – that it gives life to what couldn't truly exist without it. Ever since the dawn of man, human beings have relied on poets to put their most significant actions into words. This was true in Ancient Greece for Pindar, and is still true today.

But Angelou also showed how a black woman, belonging to a group that throughout American history has so often been humiliated, deprived of their dignity and alienated, could reclaim poetry, the loftiest form of culture, and share it with everyone. I cannot look at images from this event without tears coming to my eyes, as the moment was so hugely important.

Poetry's power to affirm life

The genius of Maya Angelou is her immeasurable confidence in poetry's power as a life-affirming force. She tells us that this is how she found the strength to hold her head high. Her autobiography, written in seven volumes, beginning with *I Know Why the Caged Bird Sings*, follows her path along what the ancients would have called a hero's journey. The young Maya Angelou, frequently targeted with racist insults, suffered from a lack of confidence. Little by little, she learns to protect her dignity and freedom, and to understand that she should not feel inferior. In other words, she describes for us how her personal and social transformation began, and invites us to experience it for ourselves.

As she writes in one of her most famous poems:

Pretty women wonder where my secret lies.
I'm not cute or built to suit a fashion model's size.
But when I start to tell them,
They think I'm telling lies.
I say,
It's in the reach of my arms,

The span of my hips,
The stride of my step,
The curl of my lips.
I'm a woman
Phenomenally.
Phenomenal woman,
That's me.

Maya Angelou says that she is a phenomenal woman because every human being is extraordinary, not because they have a particular talent or unique quality. No, it's the simple fact of being human that makes us extraordinary. In allowing ourselves just to be, separate from our successes and failures, we find the shining treasure of humanity, which lives in us all.

For me, it is poetry that teaches us this lesson and I've always thought that it is philosophy's responsibility to listen to it with humility.

A meditation on confidence – you are extraordinary

You must also learn not to apologise for just being.

We can apologise for doing something wrong, but not simply for existing. No one should feel guilty for being.

It is certainly no easy task. To help you, think of one of your attributes, no matter how simple, or think about a time when you were kind or generous. Maybe you helped a neighbour, assisted a colleague, lent a hand to a stranger. It doesn't matter what. Be proud of it – that act is the gateway to your intrinsic dignity. This is not just an abstract theory, but a real experience. A fundamental, poetic experience.

You are extraordinary.

'CHARITY IS STILL
WOUNDING FOR HIM WHO
HAS ACCEPTED IT'
MARCEL MAUSS

Doing away with moralism and good intentions

We're often encouraged to be charitable, generous, altruistic even. And more often than not, we're accused of never being charitable or generous enough. What if we got rid of these expectations? Rest assured, I am not encouraging you to become selfish and indifferent to the needs of others. But I do wish to ask a simple question: why is charity wounding to him who has accepted it?

A friend invites you to dinner

A friend invites you to have dinner at a restaurant – their treat. You accept, but insist on paying for the wine, as a token of thanks. Wouldn't it be almost the same as if you had just split the bill? Not at all. This way, each of you has offered a gift to the other.

Why did a certain friend of mine, who frequently does volunteer work, feel the need to explain: 'I'm only giving back what I have been given in life; I've received so much'? It's as if she wanted to show me that what she was doing was nothing special. Why are we so afraid of being indebted to each other? Why do we feel compelled to give in return when we receive something?

If we were only driven by monetary motives or power, then we surely would not do this. So, there is something else at play here that is more important to us than accumulating capital: our relationships with others. This is what allows us to understand the reality of our existence more deeply and why charity is so painful; a gift we cannot return isolates us, it cuts us off from others. It deprives us of the anchor of our relationships.

A meditation on gratitude

Picture this: you give a box of chocolates to a colleague who has done you a huge favour. This simple gesture has a much greater philosophical meaning. It reveals that our perception of giving as a pure and selfless act is false.

It is not because you wanted to thank him that your gift is not a real gift. It conveys something very important: that you care about this person and your relationship with him.

We tend to think that the right way to love and to give is selflessly. And in so doing we value the ideal of self-sacrifice. But, in reality, this ideal is false, dishonest and unhealthy. There is no such thing as pure love. There is no such thing as selfless charity. And thank goodness.

It is time we recognise that we are always beholden to each other in some way. This realisation has many consequences. It reveals the root of the violence plaguing our society. For example, to pay someone a modest salary, without acknowledging who they are, their commitment, or the value of their time is an act of violence. It is to deny their humanity. And all the studies back this up. The best way of preventing burnout is to acknowledge the contribution of our collaborators. To be able to give. To give back. To give thanks.

Marcel Mauss was quite right: 'Charity is wounding for him who receives it.'

It is time for us to reckon with the social, political and ethical consequences of this. We exist in relation to one another. We are not just capital to be managed.

'TO BE IN SPAIN IS
SUFFICIENT TO BE CURED
OF THE DESIRE TO
BUILD CASTLES'
MADAME DE SÉVIGNÉ

No more daydreams

'Building castles in Spain' is an old French expression that dates back to the 13th century. The phrase originated because, in Spain, there were no castles in the countryside, so the retreating Moors couldn't find shelter during the Reconquista. This expression has become a metaphor for unrealistic or impossible feats. We all dream of what we think would make us happy. But these dreams just cut us off from reality, making us unhappier.

Having this attitude is like believing that somewhere there's some all-powerful, cosmic fairy godmother who could wave her magic wand and take care of us, protect us and solve all of our problems. Religion sometimes reduces God to such a childish figure. In the political realm, figures like Stalin and Hitler were presented as saviours who could solve all of their people's problems.

You're a tech addict

Today, the castles in Spain flicker across our iPhone screens. Apps of all sorts promise to 'improve our life'. We need to 'buy this', 'look like that', 'be like this', 'weigh that much'. Yet we remain unhappy and rates of depression have reached an all-time high. And still we're told that if we have this, or we do that, then we can achieve inner peace.

Madame de Sévigné's great wisdom was to reveal the illusion: there are no castles in Spain. Once you figure this out, you're free. The problem is believing in this mirage, believing that the absence of something is the cause of your insecurity. This pseudo-infinity we're searching for can never satisfy us, it can only reinforce our anxiety. It keeps us from enjoying what we have.

A meditation on fulfilment

How do we distinguish our desire to grow, to change and to learn from this illusion of happiness?

Try taking a trip, making the effort not just to go for the sake of going but to think about what will really make the trip a success. We don't often take the time to consider what exactly we want to experience. Instead, we are under the impression that we have to do everything.

We'll do Venice in two days and Thailand in a week. And we return feeling like everything went by far too quickly.

But what would you find fulfilling? Looking at a particular painting? Meeting people? Being reunited with a friend? Taking walks in nature, deciding to do nothing at all?

Defining what you want from a trip will completely change what you will experience and will allow you to feel a profound satisfaction.

For therein lies the key. In order to be fulfilled, our journey has to have what philosophers call a finality – that is, a direction and a timeline.

Yes, imposing limits, far from constraining you, is what can make you really happy!

'FOOLISHNESS IS WANTING
TO DRAW CONCLUSIONS'
GUSTAVE FLAUBERT

How to stay curious

Conclusions seem necessary. At some point, we have to stop procrastinating, settle on a view and move on. Why does Flaubert disagree? Because by wanting to conclude, by closing the door to further discussion, deciding it's over and done with and there's nothing more to say or think about it, we set the situation in stone.

Science proves his point. Scientists work tirelessly without ever drawing definitive conclusions. Any conclusions they come to, by nature of scientific research, are provisionary. Thus, to be scientific, truth must be questionable. Otherwise, it is dogma, not truth.

Our theories about the formation of the universe, for example, are far from definitive. They only reflect the extent to which we understand the laws of physics today. In the future, when we understand physics differently, scientists will update our current theories. Then, of course, future scientists will update those theories. And so on.

To conclude is, in a sense, to stop thinking.

You are angry with your spouse

You're having an argument with your spouse. One day, your spouse tells you that they plan to quit their job and start something new. You mainly think about how risky their decision is and you dismiss it as a whim.

Your desire to draw this conclusion freezes the situation. You just want to show your spouse why they are wrong. The situation deteriorates and, before you know it, you are in a full-blown fight.

Do you want to make peace with them? It's very simple: ask them more about this new project. Find out what excites them about it. Most likely, you will discover that you failed to understand and recognise the deeper motivation pushing them to quit.

A little bit of philosophy goes a long way, especially in a situation as everyday as an argument with your spouse. Not by giving us psycho-babble advice, but by elucidating the truths underlying every relationship.

The desire to draw conclusions sets us on the path to hate and violence. When we decide that we have arrived at a conclusion, we project our own understanding onto the world and onto others, with all its prejudice, impatience and blindness. Countless political, religious and interpersonal conflicts can be explained this way. So, too, can our inability to fully reckon with climate change and the destruction of our planet. We will never be able to change direction if we continue reacting and drawing conclusions in the same way we always have.

A meditation on uncertainty

In order to change, we have to learn to embrace uncertainty. This is why we need new meditation techniques, ones that do not anaesthetise us or tell us to stay calm, but that can teach us how to sustain the discomfort of not knowing.

Imagine you don't know whether to choose Option A or Option B. Stay there for a minute. Sit and observe your doubt. Understand that you want to reach a conclusion quickly not because you want to solve your problems, but so that you don't have to worry about it any more. This is what you must teach yourself not to do. When you hastily jump to conclusions, you will always make a bad decision. Keep an open mind, be on the lookout, stay alert. The longer you stay in that uncomfortable uncertainty, the more clearly you will see your way out of any dilemma. This is what intelligence is.

In the long run, you'll see that this attitude is not as unpleasant as you might find it initially. Instead, it will open your mind to more effective, fair and, therefore, happy outcomes.

'THE KEY TO
UNDERSTANDING REALITY
IS LOSING YOURSELF IN IT'
JOHANN GOTTLIEB FICHTE

Lose yourself

Fichte, like his contemporaries Kant and Reinhold, was an extraordinary German philosopher at the end of the 18th century. One of the fundamental questions he sought to answer was how philosophy could avoid one of its biggest pitfalls: forgetting that human beings exist in relation to the world, objects and other people.

It is in this vein that Fichte wrote the following dialogue:

In the moment when you are reading a book, considering an object's beauty or speaking with a friend, are you thinking about the fact that you are reading something, considering something, hearing or seeing something?

Certainly not. I never think about myself or my own actions in those moments. I lose myself completely in the book, the object or the conversation. Thus, we also rightly say that we are absorbed by what we do or that we are immersed in it.

Fichte's remarks are convincing. The proof that you exist in relation to reality is that, at times, you yourself fade into the background. In other words, you are not what is important in these moments.

The experience of drinking a glass of water

To help you understand this experience and Fichte's philosophy, I invite you to perform the following experiment. Pour yourself a glass of water and drink it. Now, pour yourself another glass of water but, this time, look at yourself in a mirror while you drink it. Try to be as conscious as possible of the fact that you are drinking a glass of water. Suddenly, everything feels out of place, suffocating, even. It's like an ingrown toenail. As it turns back in on itself, the nail burrows into your flesh and causes you pain.

Do you know the story of the centipede and the snail? The snail asks the centipede how he manages to walk with so many feet. As soon as the centipede thinks about how he does it, he can't and comes to a standstill.

A meditation on liberating yourself from mindfulness

Over the past decade or so, I've been astonished to see the popularity of the meditation technique known as 'mindfulness' – to be as conscious as possible of everything we do at every moment in time. It makes no sense! To walk mindfully, to eat mindfully: in its strictest interpretation being mindful of everything we do is torturous and limiting.

Even more astonishing is the fact that the meditation technique I discovered over thirty years ago has explicitly freed me from this so-called 'mindfulness'. I believe that a meditation that teaches us to allow our consciousness to fade into the background is the most effective kind of meditation. The world, my surroundings and my fellow human beings are able to appear much more fully. And this shift, forgetting ourselves, is what makes us happy.

A midwife once confided in me the following wisdom: 'In my work, there are some very, very stressful moments. It feels like I need four hands and fifteen brains to keep everything straight. But it's strange – during those kinds of emergencies, it's like flipping a switch. Everything I need to do just happens, one task after another, always in the right order.' I couldn't have said it better myself.

We've all had this experience. We never really know how or why but, sometimes, what we're supposed to do just happens all by itself. We surrender ourselves to the situation and learn to trust our instincts. I believe that that is the definition of true happiness.

'ONLY HE WHO DESCENDS
INTO THE UNDERWORLD
WILL RESCUE HIS BELOVED'
SØREN KIERKEGAARD

Face your difficulties with courage

This quote from the Danish philosopher Kierkegaard recalls the myth of Orpheus, one of the most touching in history. Orpheus, a young man, does what no living being had done before him: he travels through Hades' underworld in search of his beloved Eurydice, who dies from a snakebite on their wedding day. Orpheus completes his journey thanks to his beautiful music and poetry, written out of love for Eurydice, which convinces the formidable guards to let him pass unscathed.

In other cultures, there are myths of heroes, like Gilgamesh, who travel to the depths of hell. But in each one, the hero is searching for immortality. Orpheus is the only hero who travelled to the depths of hell for love. It was love that gave him the courage and the determination to face his fears and continue through his pain.

In Kierkegaard's opinion, each one of us must descend into hell if we want to fully realise the beauty of our own humanity.

You learn that your child
is being bullied at school

Consider, for example, that your child is being bullied at school. The idea that you should remain calm and collected is absurd and counterproductive. In fact, the more we tell people that they ought to remain calm, the more unhappy they become and the more completely we alienate them. When your child tells you, in tears, that they can't take it any more, you become upset and, all of a sudden, your love for them prepares you to go through hell and back on their behalf. You are not afraid because you know you must rescue the one you love.

Of course, the one you love is simply a metaphor for everything you care strongly about, whether it's someone who's suffering, someone who's being humiliated, humanity being threatened by relentless industrialisation or our planet being destroyed every day by the blind pursuit of profit.

Another takeaway from the myth of Orpheus is that we should not travel to Hades to stay and suffer masochistically. The point is simply to pass through. This is very different. Why is this crucial to remember? Because the great problem we all encounter is to know how to handle both the descent into hell and the loved one we have come to save.

A meditation on mustering your courage

How can we find the courage to make such a difficult journey? You have to face up to your fears. It is as simple as it is unsettling: the courageous person is not one without fear, but one who is ready to meet their fear face to face, who feels pain and loses their way.

A coward doesn't want to be afraid. They don't want to be afraid for their bullied child and so will refuse to help them. Courage, therefore, means accepting vulnerability, feeling helpless, while confronting reality head-on and with a strong heart. It means not resisting these feelings.

Rather than cutting ourselves off from our own tenderness, let's embrace it.

'EVIDENCE EXHAUSTS THE
TRUTH'
GEORGES BRAQUE

Feeling loved without needing proof

One of the most prevalent assumptions of our time is that something can only be true if it can be proven. Therefore, the only two fields in which truth can be legitimately proven to us are science and law. Researchers in both fields look for proof that establishes truth based on evidence. However, there are a great many legitimate truths that are not scientific or judicial in nature. We have a tendency to neglect or even to deny them.

Georges Braque, who was a painter, knew this all too well. Oftentimes, a painting is difficult to complete and the artist must leave it for a while before they return to it. And even then, there's no guarantee of success. Perhaps they will have to leave it and return to it several times – perhaps it will never be finished. Proving that a painting is complete is, by all accounts, impossible.

Of course, this does not mean that there are no complete or beautiful paintings. What, then, are the criteria by which an artist knows their painting is finished?

Well, firstly, there are criteria that belong specifically to painting: the use of colour and materials, the harmony of forms and figures, the laws of composition, spatial orientation . . . But also how the work moves or unsettles the viewer. A masterpiece is not just a success visually – it must also move you, maybe overwhelm you. In a way, it should help you live.

What happens with paintings happens with everything that concerns our existence. For example, I want to know if you love me. Definitive proof of your answer does not exist. But that does not mean that your love cannot be true.

You are upset because one of your parents is ill

Let's do an exercise. You are feeling bereft at the moment – one of your parents has taken ill. You could search for biological, social or religious explanations for why you are feeling this way, but that won't help. We tend to feel that explaining the reasoning behind our problems will help us to resolve them. On the contrary, more often than not, looking for proof of our hardships only makes them harder.

Instead, I would suggest that you try to experience the truth of your grief. You will quickly understand that not all pain, physical or emotional, must be healed. Sometimes, the only thing that helps is being honest with yourself about what you are feeling.

You see, it is quite liberating simply to know that there is truth in our emotions, in our feelings.

A meditation on encountering your feelings

When we find ourselves experiencing the most intimate, profound and essential emotions, trying to prove or reason with them only obscures the truth of their effect on us. We would do better not to think so much about these experiences, but to trust that what we feel is true.

You can learn to truly appreciate a work of art or truly listen to a piece of music in the same way – by simply letting yourself experience the depth, the quality and the sincerity of the effect that it has on you. You see, the kind of truth Braque mentions cannot be proven or demonstrated. Nevertheless, it is a truth that engages and informs our entire existence.

Yes, Georges Braque was right: 'Evidence exhausts the truth.'

'SAIL YOUR SHIP AWAY
FROM SUCH HIGH WINDS
AND STORMY SWELLS'
ARISTOTLE

Morals without doctrine

Aristotle, the father of moral philosophy, cites this passage from Homer's *Odyssey* to help him to define 'morals'.

Being a person of morals does not mean, despite our modern misunderstandings, that one must always follow certain rules or commandments to the letter. Rather, living a moral life is like sailing a ship. A good sailor must know how to avoid two dangerous extremes: high winds and dangerous sea swells. He must learn how to stay the course while turning sometimes this way, sometimes that way, in order to benefit from the most helpful winds and currents.

In life, we face similar dilemmas. How can I say no, without seeming cowardly or aggressive? Have I said too much? Or not enough?

When I was a student, I found this approach to morality rather lacklustre. I was expecting to find something much more enlightening in moral philosophy. Now, however, I fully appreciate the heroism that is required to always strike the right balance.

What I have come to understand is that being a just, moral person does not always mean living in the middle of two extremes. Having the perfect balance of hot and cold, like lukewarm water, is not acting morally. Rather, acting with balanced morals means existing at the most dizzying intersection of experience and circumstance, like a dancer whose movements take the audience's breath away or a doctor who knows how to take into consideration every detail while making a diagnosis.

Having had my share of difficulties and crises, I am better able to understand how illuminating this approach can be.

You must give your friend some bad news

You have been tasked with breaking difficult news to a close friend. You are very anxious. You are afraid of hurting your friend and don't know how they'll take it. You would like to know how to do it; you would like someone to shepherd you. This is misguided. The situation is more delicate than that. You must remember what Aristotle calls contingency: the world is not pre-programmed. In other words, shit happens. It's painful. We have to acknowledge this. And doing so is already a first step.

Believing that everything we experience should be in some way agreeable paradoxically makes us feel sad, and above all powerless. Living means learning how to sail on troubled waters, how to make tough decisions. Since the world is not perfect, it is up to us to perfect it. To try to do our best.

In reality, you will never know whether the manner in which you chose to approach a situation was really the best one. But that's not the point. Living isn't about solving equations.

A meditation on the art of sailing

Okay, but how do I break this bad news to my friend? The secret is to continue to examine the situation with utmost care. When would be the best moment to take my friend aside? How should I start the conversation? Should I talk to him by myself, or should I ask another friend to help me? By asking yourself these and other questions, you will discover how best to navigate the situation.

Aristotle teaches us to put aside the opposition of good and evil and instead to look for that marvellous balance somewhere between the two extremes. In this way, he teaches us flexibility and agility.

'LOVE NEVER DIES A NATURAL DEATH. IT DIES BECAUSE WE DON'T KNOW HOW TO REPLENISH ITS SOURCE'
ANAÏS NIN

The wonderful and mysterious art
of knowing how to love

They say that love has built-in obsolescence, that it will inevitably be worn out by routine and daily wear. The initial intensity of love is but a passing moment and we must resign ourselves to that fact.

For Anaïs Nin, a brilliant woman, and a friend to Antonin Artaud and Henry Miller, this is a completely false understanding. Put simply, for Nin, love is not an immediate and reciprocated ecstatic passion; it is a mistake to associate love with pleasure.

Love is hard work: it's a challenge that implicates our entire existence. But it is this work that can make us deeply happy.

If you're having trouble in love, with your child, your partner, your parents . . .

Think of someone you love, but with whom something feels blocked, frozen or tense. It could be your child, your partner or one of your parents.

Instead of feeling overcome by resentment or injustice, it's time to learn how to work at love. This might make you feel uncomfortable because you associate work with a massive effort – and you know all too well that you can't force yourself to love. But rest assured, it's not a question of forcing it. So, what does it mean, then, to work at loving one another?

You should always be open, attentive. A mother has to work at loving her child – we must rid ourselves of the damaging idea that a mother knows how to love her child perfectly from the moment that child is born. On the contrary, we have to know how to 'replenish its source', as Anaïs Nin says. But how?

It's here that the idea of a source is illuminating. A spring is not stable and set in place. It gives of itself in a gush, gives without asking for anything in return, without checking if we are ready to receive it or not. It is not like a bank account that I can manage as I like, but rather it demands that I remain open to receive it.

A meditation on love

Loving is an art. We can acquire this art by meditating on how to learn to feel. It's hard because we spend a lot of time trying not to feel anything, trying to stay on top of everything, to stay in control, to remain unmoved. However, we have to try. Think again of your child or your partner. Allow yourself to be touched, either because they irritate you or they move you – it doesn't matter.

Voilà. The important thing is to tap into your own tenderness, your own generosity, because there and there alone can you replenish the source of your love.

'WHEN I HAVEN'T ANY
BLUE, I USE RED'
PABLO PICASSO

How to reach a decision

This Pablo Picasso quote might seem overly simple. But really, it isn't. By using red instead of blue, you're not using one colour instead of another, but rather accepting that sometimes you have to rethink entirely. Picasso knew that painting is composition – figuring out how to put elements together.

Composition is a painter's term but, in our lives, we practise composition all the time because we constantly have to make decisions while taking several parameters into account: who to invite to dinner, or what activity our kids will enjoy most based on the weather.

If we get discouraged and stop working because we've run out of blue, it's because we've made everything rigid. We have mistakenly believed that there is only one way out and, if that way is blocked, then we're done for. But, in reality, that's never the case. There are always other options that we haven't yet envisioned.

You were planning on staying with friends this summer and suddenly they announce they can't host you any more

You had planned on visiting some friends this summer. Everything had been agreed and then they call, distressed, telling you that you can't stay with them any more – a sick child, an unexpected leak, a death in the family . . . You're devastated. So, what do you do? Remember Picasso. When he hasn't got any blue, he uses red. Don't try to completely overhaul your plans – recompose your summer. And a door may open that will surprise you.

Philosophically, it's a fascinating idea because this is where the lost feeling of freedom resides. We believe today that being free means doing what we want. But if I yell at someone because I'm angry, does the yelling make me feel freer? No. You are free because you are not bound to a set of mechanical, habitual behaviours. You are free because you can see the situation clearly for what it is. You are free because you are ready to take what it is and compose with it.

A meditation on creativity

Now try to learn this subtle art. Take an ordinary situation: the meal you're making for dinner, or a presentation you must prepare. Your first reflex is to brainstorm new ideas. Before you know it, you're stuck. You can't do it. What if you followed Picasso's example and learned the art of composition?

To do this, examine the situation closely: what do you have in your kitchen store cupboard? Which foods and which spices? Maybe these will provide you with inspiration. You can also go to the market, paying attention to ingredients that are in season. This way, you'll learn creativity by changing your perspective and looking at reality from several different angles. When you haven't any blue, you'll use red. And it will be marvellous.

SOURCES

1. George Orwell, *The Collected Essays, Journalism and Letters of George Orwell Vol IV: In Front of Your Nose, 1945–50* (London: Secker & Warburg, 1968).
2. Albert Camus, *Personal Writings* (London: Vintage, 2020). Used by permission of Vintage Books, an imprint of Penguin Publishing Group, a division of Penguin Random House LLC. All rights reserved.
3. Paul Celan, 'Corona' in *Poems of Paul Celan*, trans. Michael Hamburger (London: Anvil Press Poetry, 2007). Reprinted by kind of permission of Carcanet Press, Manchester, UK.
4. Emil Cioran, *La Chute Dans Le Temps* (Paris: Gallimard, 1990). Author translation.
5. Emily Dickinson, 'Water is Taught by Thirst', *The Complete Works of Emily Dickinson* (London: Little Brown, 1976).
6. Erasmus, *Éloge de la Folie*, ed. Maurice Rat, trans. Pierre de Nolhac (Paris: Flammarion, 2016).

7. Attributed to Johann Wolfgang von Goethe.
8. *Heraclite*, trans. Jean Brun (Paris: Éditions Seghers, 1965).
9. Immanuel Kant, *Critique de la Raison Pratique* (Paris: François Picave, 1921).
10. Lou Andreas Salomé, *Le Narcissisme* (Paris: Presses Universitaires de France, 2002).
11. Rainer Maria Rilke, *Lettres à une Jeune Poète*, VIII (Paris: Grasset, 2002).
12. Olga Sedakova, *Éditions l'Age d'Homme* (Paris: Petite Bibliothèque Slave, 2001).
13. Henri Matisse, *Écrits et propos sur l'art* (Paris: Éditions Hermann, 1978).
14. Max Jacob, *Esthétique; Lettres à René Guy Cadou (1937–1944)* (Nantes: Joca Seria, 2001).
15. Henri Michaux, *Poteaux d'angle* (Paris: Gallimard, 2004).
16. Nelly Sachs, *Lettres en Provenance de la Nuit*, trans. Bernard Pautrat (Paris: Allia, 2010).
17. Samuel Beckett, 'Worstward Ho' in *Company / Ill Seen Ill Said / Worstward Ho / Stirrings Still* (London: Faber & Faber, 2009).
18. Henri Bergson, *L'Évolution créatrice* (Paris: Éditions Felix Alcan, 1907).
19. Simone de Beauvoir, *The Ethics of Ambiguity* (New York: Philosophical Library LLC/Open Road, 2015).

20. Gertrude Stein, *Selected Writings by Gertrude Stein* (New York: Vintage, 1990).

21. Marc Bloch, *Strange Defeat*, trans. Gerard Hopkins (New York: Norton, 1968).

22. Charles Baudelaire, *Fusées, Mon Cœur Mis à Nu*, ed. Andre Guyaux (Paris: Gallimard, 2016).

23. Ludwig Wittgenstein, 'Lecture on Ethics', ed. Edoardo Zamuner, Ermelinda Valentina Di Lascio and D.K. Levy (London: Wiley-Blackwell, 2014).

24. Marina Tsvetaeva, *L'Art à la Lumière De La Conscience*, trans. Véronique Lossky (Paris: Le Temps Qu'il Fait, 1998).

25. Plato, *The Apology of Socrates*.

26. Simone Weil, *Réflexions sur le Bon Usage des Études Scolaires en Vue de l'Amour de Dieu* (Paris: Omnia Poche, 2018).

27. Hannah Arendt, *Between Past and Future* (London: Viking Books, 1968). Used by permission of Viking Books, an imprint of Penguin Publishing Group, a division of Penguin Random House LLC. All rights reserved.

28. Friedrich Nietzsche, *Ecce Homo*, trans. R.J. Hollingdale (London: Penguin Classics, 1992).

29. Toni Morrison, 'Voir Comme on ne Voit Jamais', interview by Pierre Bourdieu, *Vacarme*, Winter 1998, pp. 58–60, varame.org.

30. James Baldwin, 'They Can't Turn Back' (1960).

31. Maya Angelou, *Rainbow in the Cloud: The Wit and Wisdom of Maya Angelou* (London: Virago, 2016). Poetry in this chapter from: Maya Angelou, 'Phenomenal Woman' from *And Still I Rise* (London: Virago, 2013).

32. Marcel Mauss, *Sociologie et Anthropologie* (Paris: Presses Universitaires de France, 2013).

33. Madame de Sévigné, *Letters 1646–1696* (Paris: Librairie de Firmin Didot Freres, 1846).

34. Gustave Flaubert, Letter to Louis Bouilhet, Damascus, 4 September 1850.

35. Johann Gottlieb Fichte, *Rapport Clair Comme Le Jour Adressé au Grand Public sur le Caractère Propre de la Philosophie Nouvelle (1801) et Autres Textes*, trans. Pierre-Philippe Druet et Auguste Valensin (France: Librairie philosophique J. Vrin, 1986).

36. Søren Kierkegaard, *Crainte et Tremblement* (France: Aubier, 1984).

37. Georges Braque, *Le Jour et la Nuit* (Paris: Gallimard, 1952).

38. Aristotle, *The Nichomachean Ethics*.

39. Anaïs Nin, *Les Chambres du Cœur* (Paris: Editions Stock, 2003).

40. Attributed to Pablo Picasso.